ITALIAN REPATRIATION
FROM THE UNITED STATES, 1900-1914

by
Betty Boyd Caroli

CENTER FOR MIGRATION STUDIES
New York

866120

Italian Repatriation from the United States, 1900-1914

First Edition

Copyright © 1973 by
The Center for Migration Studies of New York, Inc.

Center for Migration Studies
209 Flagg Place
Staten Island, N. Y. 10304

ISBN 0-913256-10-2
Library of Congress Catalog Card Number: 73-85825
Printed in the United States of America

TABLE OF CONTENTS

PREFACE.. V

ILLUSTRATIONS.................................... VII

TABLES... VII

CHAPTER

I. Repatriation as a Factor in American
   History 3
II. Extent and Characteristics of Italian
   Repatriation from the United States 23

III. Reaction of the Italian Government to
   Repatriation from the United States
   between 1902 and 1914 as Reported in
   the *Bollettino dell'Emigrazione* 51
IV. Repatriates' Impressions of the United
   States, 1900-1914 73
V. Conclusions 91

BIBLIOGRAPHY 101

PREFACE

This study examines Italian repatriation from the United States between 1900 and 1914. Although Italians, as well as Greeks, Germans and Britons, left America in large numbers at different times, their reemigration has escaped extensive study by historians, economists and sociologists. Those scholars in each field who have dealt with repatriation have disagreed on its causes and effects, although they have concurred in its importance to both countries involved.

More than 1.5 million Italians left the United States in the first 15 years of the twentieth century. Before 1903 Italian government reports deemphasized the magnitude of repatriation to the peninsula even though Americans repeatedly objected to the "birds of passage." By 1904 Italian officials admitted that hundreds of thousands of Italy's workers sought temporary employment in America each year while their families remained in the *paese*.

The *Bollettino dell'Emigrazione* reported numerous advantages to be derived from the arrangement. The United States served as a safety valve for Italy's unemployed workers and became the source of millions of dollars of remittances sent back by workers to their families, creditors and bank accounts. The two-way travel across the Atlantic also boosted Italy's developing shipping industry.

Most of the educated repatriates who wrote of their residence in the United States between 1900 and 1914 praised many aspects of life in America, although they criticized others. The experiences of the less educated workers, more typical members of the mass migration, generally escaped being recorded. Those returned laborers who consented to interviews with me spoke enthusiastically of their years in America. The new country gave them jobs, they pointed out, when Italy could not. Temporary emigration was their own solution, they said, to economic problems which they faced as individuals. They seemed unaware of the actions of the Italian government to facilitate their return to Italy by reducing costs of parts of the return journey, by subsidizing agencies in America which fostered ties between Italians abroad and their native land and by making resumption of Italian citizenship easier.

v

Although I have had the help of many persons, the conclusions I have reached are my own. I have used Italian sources extensively, and the translations of those materials which appear in the following pages are also mine. Most of the repatriates whom I interviewed insisted on anonymity, and I have respected their wishes by assigning them pseudonyms. Discussing their experiences with these people, even though their memories may be of limited significance and questionable accuracy, contributed to my own picture of the reemigration experience. I wish to thank Domenico Rossi, Giuseppe and Anna Tito who helped locate these repatriates. Livio Caroli assisted in all the interviews.

The research in Italy was made possible by a grant under the Fulbright-Hays Act. Cipriana Scelba and Luigi Filadoro, of the Commissione per gli Scambi Culturali in Rome, were especially helpful in organizing my work in Italy. I used several libraries in Rome, including the *Biblioteca Nazionale* and the Emigration Collection at the *Ministero degli Affari Esteri*. The major part of my research was completed at the *Centro di Studi Emigrazione*, and I wish to thank particularly Reverend Giovanni Sacchetti, C.S. and Reverend Gian Fausto Rosoli, C.S., both of the Center, for their aid in locating materials. Dorothy Swanson and Ronald Tempest read sections of the manuscript, and I am grateful for their suggestions.

Betty Boyd Caroli

ILLUSTRATIONS

Illustration   *Page*

I   Italian Emigrants to the United States by Origin in
    Italy, 1884-1896   35
II Italian Repatriates from the United States in 1905-
    1906, By Destination in Italy   47

TABLES

Table   *Page*
I   Annual Average Number of Emigrants Returning to
     Italy   11
II   Italian Repatriates' Length of Residence in the
     United States   13
III Immigrants to the United States: By Age and Sex ..   15
IV   Percentage of Males Among Immigrants to the
     United States and Emigrant Aliens from the
     United States   16
V   Occupations of Emigrant Aliens from the United
     States between 1908 and 1914   17
VI   Immigration to the United States, 1820-1860   27
VII Italian Emigrants to the Americas by Section of
     Origin, 1866-1868   29
VIII Italian Emigrants to the United States in 1873   29
IX   Italian Emigration, 1876-1899   31
X   Immigration to the United States, 1861-1899   33
XI   Italians to the United States by Region of Origin,
     1876-1896   34
XII Passengers Arriving in Italian Ports in Third Class
     Accommodations, 1884-1899   37
XIII Italian Emigration, 1900-1914   38
XIV Comparison of Three Sets of Statistics on Italian
     Emigration to the United States, 1902-1906   39
XV   Italians to the United States by Origin, 1906-1909   40

Table   *Page*

XVI   Passengers Arriving in Italian Ports in Third Class Accommodations, 1900-1914 41

XVII   Percentage of Emigrants from Each Region Applying to Local Registries for Reinstatement after Residence Abroad 42

XVIII   Italian Emigrant Aliens from the United States between 1908 and 1914: By Occupation 44

XIX   Italians Returning from the United States in 1905-1906: By Age and Sex 45

XX   Italians Arriving in Italian Ports in 1906 48

XXI   Italian Repatriates from the United States in 1905-1906: By Sex and Destination in Italy 48

XXII   Italian Repatriates from the United States in 1905-1906 Compared to Emigrants in 1901-1902 and 1905-1906: By Region 49

XXIII   Remittances Made Through the *Banco di Napoli* by Italian Emigrants, 1902-1914: By Method of Transmission 58

XXIV   Remittances from Italian Emigrants in the United States Compared to Total Remittances Through the *Banco di Napoli* 59

XXV   Reported Rate of Illness and Death among Italians Traveling Third Class between Italy and the United States, 1903-1906 67

XXVI   Number of Cases Treated among Italians in Third Class Travel between the United States and Italy in 1904 68

XXVII   Share of Total Strikes and Participants in Various Regions of Italy, 1904-1914 94

XXVIII   *Lire* Held in Italian Banks by Italians Resident in Italy and Abroad 96

XXIX   Value of Exports from Italy and Imports to Italy, 1901-1913 97

ITALIAN REPATRIATION FROM THE UNITED STATES, 1900-1914

1

**Repatriation as
a Factor in
American History**

MILLIONS OF immigrants to the United States were only temporary Americans. Neither refused nor necessarily rejected by the new country, they returned of their own volition to the land they had left. Sometimes the repatriation occurred after a few months; in other cases it took place after several years or even as much as half a lifetime. Estimates of the total number of repatriates range from less than ten percent of the total immigration to America in the years before 1860 to more than 100 percent of some nationality groups in selected years after 1900.[1] Not officially recorded by the United States Office of Immigration until 1908, departing aliens, nevertheless, probably had constituted for several decades a large portion of passengers on ships sailing from Atlantic ports. The Commissioner of Immigration estimated in 1910 that for many years the number of alien residents leaving annually had been about one-third as great as the number that arrived.[2] Statistics indicate that for every 100 immigrants to America between 1908 and 1924, approximately 38 repatriated.[3]

If the estimates of the Commissioner for the period before 1908 and his reports for the following years are accepted, American historians have another chapter to add to the melting pot controversy. For the millions who settled in the United States only temporarily, the question was not how to be accepted in the new country but whether to adapt to it or not. While the Americanizers were preaching the easiest routes to assimilation and their opponents were suggesting the advantages of a culturally pluralistic society, the immigrants were raising their own questions about the desirability of either.

Students of American immigration have, with few exceptions, neglected what was for many persons the second, and final, move. Concentrating on the changes permanent immigrants produced on America or those which the adopted country exerted on the newcomers, historians have avoided the cases which illustrated neither. Investigation of repatriation shows that it continued through three centuries of American settlement.

William L. Sachse, historian of seventeenth-century England,

___

[1] Simon Kuznets and Ernest Rubin, *Immigration and the Foreign Born* (New York, 1954), 22-3; Walter F. Willcox, *International Migrations* (2 vols., New York, 1929-1931), II, 624.

[2] U.S. Immigration Commission, 1907-1910, *Reports of the Immigration Commission* (41 vols., Washington, 1911), III, 373.

[3] Willcox, *International Migrations*, I, 206.

examined the movement of persons from America to England between 1640 and 1660, two decades in which departures from the New World outnumbered arrivals.[4] After looking at writings of persons who discussed their return to England during those years, Sachse concluded that the motivations were diverse but that the decision to leave was an individual or family choice rather than the result of organization or group effort.[5] Repatriates cited different causes for their return: the economic depression of the 1640's, the rigid political and religious system which rejected some potential settlers as unworthy, and the chance to profit from old connections who had come to power in England.[6] Those remaining in America showed more concern for the quality of the people who left than for their numbers.[7] In 1641-42, for example, 14 of the 114 university-educated men living in New England left the colonies, and several of them relinquished positions of leadership to return to what they considered better opportunities.[8] Once back in England, they usually remained even after the reestablishment of the monarchy caused an increase in emigration in the 1660's.[9]

English reemigration from America did not terminate with the Restoration. Wilbur Shepperson, another student of British population change, estimated that substantial numbers of disappointed Englishmen continued to leave America throughout the eighteenth and nineteenth centuries.[10] Basing his conclusions on British Board of Trade records and on reports of the United States Commissioner of Immigration, Shepperson wrote that 370,697 former British and Irish nationals reemigrated from the United States in the 1880's.[11] In just one year of that decade, 1889, a total of 240,395 Britons entered the United States, but 71,392 departed the same year, leaving a net immigration approximately 25 percent less than the gross.[12] The large return movement did not terminate in the nineteenth century. It continued into the twentieth. In 1931 twice

---

[4] William L. Sachse, "The Migration of New Englanders to England, 1640-60," *American Historical Review*, LIII (January 1948), 251.

[5] *Ibid.*, 259.

[6] *Ibid.*, 252-8.

[7] *Ibid.*, 260.

[8] *Ibid.*

[9] *Ibid.*, 278.

[10] Wilbur S. Shepperson, *Emigration and Disenchantment* (Norman, 1965), 4-5.

[11] *Ibid.*, 5.

[12] *Ibid.*

as many Englishmen left America as came, and in the following year, while the Great Depression continued, the British repatriation rate doubled.[13]

Motives compelling the British to return differed, Shepperson wrote, from those which drew other immigrant groups back to their countries. A heterogeneous group of individuals with a broad range of occupations and abilities, the immigrants from the British Isles did not suffer the group prejudice or language barriers that the Greeks and Italians found. Shepperson wrote:

> The British seldom left the United States because of congestion, trouble with the law, labor organization difficulties, nativist discrimination, or resentment of their religion, speech, color or culture. They were not one of the submerged minorities. But since the British found immigration a less disruptive ordeal than other Europeans, by the same token, they were better equipped to understand and judge America, make sharp comparisons, and indulge in enlightened criticism.[14]

The repatriation rate for Englishmen was particularly high among those who had traveled to America with some sort of financial assistance.[15] The return movement had begun, however, before monetary help became available, and Shepperson concluded that no single explanation sufficed.[16] Many of the returnees voiced disappointment with what they found in America.[17] One of the extremely disillusioned, Charles Hooton, published a book in which he explained his reasons for writing:

> I determined, if possible, while there was yet time, in some shape or other to lay my experiences of Texas before the world, and to the upmost of my ability persuade, through the influence of facts, any projecting Emigrants from following in the same fatal footsteps.[18]

Hooton lamented, "May I never again see such ruin of body and fortune, such wreck of heart, as it was my fate to witness in Texas."[19]

---

[13] *Ibid.*
[14] *Ibid.*, 7.
[15] *Ibid.*, 18.
[16] *Ibid.*,
[17] *Ibid.*, 47.
[18] Charles Hooton, *St. Louis' Isle* (London, 1847), vii.
[19] *Ibid.*, 42.

Hooton left little doubt concerning his feelings about the time he spent in America. Other Englishmen felt less strongly, but they refused to adjust to life in the new country. Shepperson concluded from case histories, for example, that a desire for upward mobility was the characteristic most commonly shared by the repatriates, yet many of them refused to change occupations in order to profit in their new land.[20] British immigrants to the United States encountered only a variation of the language, values, racial stock, climate and culture which they had left behind, but for many of those whose writings Shepperson cited, even these differences proved too great. Better able to record their disappointments than later immigrants, they left behind a sometimes bitter, often illuminating record of their sojourn.[21]

By the beginning of the twentieth century, Germans led all other nationalities in the number of foreign-born in the United States.[22] In 1900 more than one in four American residents not born in the United States reported Germany as their birthplace.[23] Alfred Vagts, the German historian, pointed out that this large group did not include the total number who had immigrated to the new country in the preceding years, because Germans, too, repatriated.[24] Between 1908, when United States immigration statistics began to include a record of departing aliens, and 1924, the number of Germans who left America amounted to about 16 for every 100 arrivals from that country.[25] Although Germans ranked below other nationality groups in the percentage who returned, a sizeable number of persons was involved.

Just as Shepperson looked at individual cases to see what motivated Britons to repatriate, Vagts examined the writings of reemigrated Germans. In the early part of the book he dealt with statistical aspects of the migration in order to isolate possible reasons for the return. Vagts' emphasis, however, was not on statistics because numbers could not explain, he noted, the immigrants' feelings about their experiences in the two countries. Vagts' findings, based

---

[20] Shepperson, *Emigration and Disenchantment*, 186.
[21] *Ibid.*, 31-196.
[22] U.S. Bureau of the Census, *Thirteenth Census of the United States Taken in the Year 1910: Abstract of the Census* (Washington, 1913), 188.
[23] *Ibid.*
[24] Alfred Vagts, *Deutsch-Amerikanische Rückwanderung: Probleme, Phänomene, Statistik, Politik, Soziologie, Biographie* (Heidelberg, 1960), 2.
[25] Willcox, *International Migrations*, II, 477.

on an examination of biographical accounts of the repatriates, their diaries, letters and travel guides, pointed to complex pressures which drew Germans back to their country. The attractions of Germany helped encourage its people to return from their very first venture to America until the time in which Vagts wrote.

Some groups from among the "new immigration" which came to America in large numbers after 1890 appear to have found even less satisfaction in their adopted country than the Germans and English had. Theodore Saloutos, the noted American historian with Hellenistic interests, discussed with Greek repatriates their experiences in order to discover why so many of them returned home.[26] Saloutos noted that between 1908 and 1931 Greeks ranked fourth, after Italians, Poles and English, in number of returnees.[27] He concentrated on the repatriation which occurred between 1908 and 1924, but especially that of 1911-1914 and 1919-1921, when Greek reemigration was heaviest.[28]

Greeks who had left America reported various motives: some felt nostalgia for the life they had had as children; others suffered economic losses in 1907 and decided America could not meet their expectations to get rich quickly; some told Saloutos that they had responded to Greek government efforts to draw them home to fight in 1912-1913; others went back to see their families, to enjoy the milder climate or to escape the impersonalization of American society.[29] Most of them were citizens of Greece when they returned.[30] The majority were men between the ages of 16 and 44 and reported a residence of five years or more in the United States.[31] Back in Greece another readjustment was necessary since many of the repatriates reported that they experienced difficulties.[32] They criticized practices which they had not objected to before leaving, and, constantly comparing Greece with the United States, they realized they were not entirely satisfied with either.

Saloutos emphasized the unrecorded but significant contributions of those who returned to Greece when he wrote:

---

[26] Theodore Saloutos, *They Remember America* (Berkeley, 1956), 88-102.

[27] *Ibid.*, 30.

[28] *Ibid.*, vii.

[29] *Ibid.*, 32-35.

[30] *Ibid.*, 51.

[31] *Ibid.*

[32] *Ibid.*, 57-73.

The repatriates who returned from the United States could not help but bring to Greece some of both the material and the intangible qualities of American life. In going from an advanced to a retarded social economy, they took with them money, higher standards of living, a spirit of optimism, reformist attitudes and pronounced pro-American sentiments. They had come into contact with a different language, with different customs and attitudes. They could hardly have failed to acquire new skills and techniques; their tempo of life had quickened; they had seen people worship in different churches; for better or for worse, they were exposed to the American press, periodicals and literature; they had seen women treated differently . . . . Even though their names failed to appear on the facades of libraries, museums and schools of Athens, their contributions were nevertheless genuine.[33]

Robert F. Foerster, the distinguished Harvard historian, was one of the first American scholars to consider in depth the temporary nature of Italian emigration.[34] Foerster wrote in 1919 that nine-tenths of the Italians who had gone to other parts of Europe had returned, and each year an increasing number of those who crossed the Atlantic turned homeward.[35] In total numbers the Italian repatriation was large. According to Foerster, between 300,000 and 400,000 nationals returned home each year between 1902 and 1914.[36] In order to arrive at these figures, Foerster used Italian reports, because countries in the Western Hemisphere did not keep careful records of departing aliens until after the movement had become large. Foerster suggested that American attempts to report the destination of its emigrants would have met with little success because of the necessity of relying solely on statements of intention. Using reports of the Italian Ministry of Marine for the years before 1901 and of emigration inspectors afterwards, Foerster concluded that the peak year for repatriation from America occurred in 1908. Table I shows that more than 300,000 Italians fled the Western Hemisphere in that 12-month period.

Searching for the causes of the reemigration, Foerster examined monographs published by the Italian government.[37]

---

[33] *Ibid.*, 130-131.

[34] Robert F. Foerster, *The Italian Emigration of Our Times* (Cambridge, 1919), 23-43.

[35] *Ibid.*, 42.

[36] *Ibid.*

[37] *Ibid.*, 23-43.

TABLE I

ANNUAL AVERAGE NUMBER OF EMIGRANTS
RETURNING TO ITALY°

Year	From the United States	From North and South America
1887-1891	5,371	37,097
1892-1896	20,075	54,622
1897-1901	26,992	72,631
1902-1906	88,012	134,457
1906	109,258	157,987
1907	176,727	248,428
1908	240,877	300,834
1909	73,806	134,210
1910	104,459	158,902
1911	154,027	216,820
1912	129,649	182,990
1913	122,589	188,978
1914	156,274	219,178

Adapted from Robert Foerster, *The Italian Emigration of Our Times* (Cambridge, 1919), 30.
° Includes persons arriving in Italian ports in third class accommodations before 1902. After that date includes only Italians arriving in those ports. Foerster estimated that if first and second class travelers had been included, the total number coming from North and South America would have been increased by 15,000 each year.

These reports indicated that the returned nationals were usually males between 16 and 45 years of age, generally unskilled workers, and traveling alone rather than with a family.[38] Foerster concluded on the basis of these reports: "The emigrants expect, in leaving Italy, not to develop ties abroad, but only to lay by dollars. And when the dollars cease to come, the return home begins."[39]

A contemporary student of Italian repatriation, Francesco P. Cerase, questioned a group of his countrymen who had returned from the United States.[40] Cerase found that, of those he surveyed, about 18 percent had reemigrated before their fifth year in America, about 24 percent had stayed between five and ten years, 17 percent between 10 and 15 years, 15 percent between 15 and 30

---

[38] *Ibid.*, 41.
[39] *Ibid.*
[40] Francesco P. Cerase, "A Study of Italian Migrants Returning from the U.S.A.," *International Migration Review*, I (Summer 1967), 67-74.

years and 26 percent had remained more than 30 years.[41] Cerase concluded that two peak periods of reemigration occurred: one after six to ten years of American residence and the other after 30 years.[42]

Cerase's findings differ from those of Foerster who reported that the overwhelming majority of those Italians who repatriated from America did so within five years of their arrival in the new country.[43] Not concerned with those who turned back in the first 12 months of their sojourn abroad, Foerster examined the remaining repatriated Italians and found that nearly four out of five had been in America fewer than five years.[44] The percentages varied from 82.0 percent in 1908 to 57.9 percent in 1916. In only two of the intervening years did fewer than 70 percent of returning Italian nationals report an American residence of one to five years.

Foerster's findings tend to be supported by the reports, partially reproduced in Table II, of the United States Commissioner General of Immigration for 1908 to 1913. Beginning with the fiscal year ending June 30, 1908, persons departing from America were questioned to ascertain their citizenship and their intentions of returning. Those who declared themselves to be Italian nationals without desire to resume American residence were included with other emigrant aliens. Table II shows that the overwhelming majority had stayed fewer than five years in the new country.

Cerase's findings of the two peak periods of repatriation, one after six to ten years and the other after 30 years, reflect the different time in which he wrote. Italian immigration to America was sharply cut by the legislation of 1921 and 1924. Since Cerase wrote in the 1960's, his respondents included many who settled in the United States after the quota legislation became effective. Foerster, writing in 1919 when immigration to America remained relatively unrestricted and could be undertaken without serious commitment, found that residence abroad had generally continued less than five years.

An examination of the work of Sachse, Shepperson, Vagts, Saloutos, Foerster and Cerase indicates the importance of reemi-

---

[41] *Ibid.*, 70.
[42] *Ibid.*
[43] Foerster, *The Italian Emigration*, 35.
[44] *Ibid.*

TABLE II

ITALIAN REPATRIATES' LENGTH OF RESIDENCE IN THE UNITED STATES

Fiscal Year Ending June 30	Total Number of Italians Departing from U.S.	Number Reporting Less Than 5 Years Residence in U.S.
1908	167,335	137,236
1909	86,439	69,978
1910	52,772	42,949
1911	76,218	59,516
1912	109,887	79,159
1913	90,052	61,177

United States Commissioner General of Immigration, *Annual Report* (Washington, 1908-1913), *passim.*

gration to American history. Investigation of the subject reveals, however, gaps in information available. The estimated 12 million persons who left the United States between 1801 and 1935 affected both countries they inhabited: religious organizations, consumption patterns, foreign affairs and job markets.[45] Historians have focused far too little attention on the consequences of this population shift.

Economists, attempting to demonstrate and explain business cycles, have considered the contribution of immigration. Some of them have included repatriation in their investigations. Students of population movements have acknowledged that any country experiencing emigration or immigration undergoes changes in its labor supply and consumer segment, as well as in other parts of its business life. The literature dealing with the economic effects on America of international population shifts is much too vast to consider here, but some outstanding treatments of the effects of arriving and departing aliens on the working force can be mentioned.

The population of the United States grew between 1870 and 1910 from 38,558,000 to 91,972,000, and immigration played no small part in this increase.[46] By the first decade of the twentieth century, immigration added nearly a million persons a year to the

---

[45] Kurt B. Mayer, Review of Alfred Vagts' *Deutsch-Amerikanische Rückwanderung: Probleme, Phänomene, Statistik, Politik, Soziologie, Biographie* in *American Sociological Review* XXVI (February 1961), 139.

[46] Harry Jerome, *Migration and Business Cycles* (New York, 1926), 49.

census.[47] In the 40 years between 1870 and 1910 one-seventh of the total population growth resulted from immigration.[48] The increase which these arrivals effected in the labor supply exceeded their contribution to the population.[49] The difference resulted from the predominance of males among the immigrants, many of them old enough to go immediately to work.[50] Since relatively few women took jobs outside the home, it is necessary to consider the large proportion of males among the arriving aliens in order to understand the impact of immigration on the labor supply.

Except for the Irish, all nationality groups immigrating to America contributed more men than women.[51] This particular aspect of migration was evident from the first statistics compiled for 1820, and the trend continued for 100 years. In no year before 1922 did the total number of arriving females exceed that of males. Since restrictive legislation went into effect in the 1920's, a majority of males has been uncommon. Table III shows the percentage of the total number which was male in any decade and gives an indication of the large numbers of those responding who were between 14 and 40 years of age.

Many possible explanations exist to account for the high percentage of males among immigrants to the United States. Young, single men, out for fame and fortune, could more easily finance a trip to the New World than their older brothers already settled down with a wife and children. The younger sons may have seen limited possibilities for themselves if they did not leave. Perhaps they accepted the prospect of a rigorous transoceanic journey with more tranquillity. In any case, the United States was not unique in this respect.

As a result of the male influx, the labor force became increasingly foreign-born after the Civil War even though the height of immigration, if expressed as a percentage of the native-born population, occurred just before 1860. In the decade between July 1, 1846 and June 30, 1855, an average of three foreigners arrived each year for every 200 native-born American residents.[52]

---

[47] *Ibid.*
[48] Kuznets and Rubin, *Immigration and the Foreign Born*, 4.
[49] *Ibid.*
[50] Jerome, *Migration and Business Cycles*, 49.
[51] *Ibid.*
[52] *Ibid.*

TABLE III

IMMIGRANTS TO THE UNITED STATES
BY AGE AND SEX

Years	Total Immigration	Percentage of Total Between 15 and 40 Years of Age	Male Percentage of Total
1820-1829	151,636	62.6	72.8
1830-1839	527,716	63.1	65.4
1840-1849	1,479,478	66.0	59.2
1850-1859	3,457,212	58.2	57.9
1860-1869	2,278,612	67.3	59.9
1870-1879	2,742,137	65.9	61.1
1880-1889	5,238,568	68.4	61.0
1890-1899	3,851,150	76.7°	61.0
1900-1909	8,202,348	82.9°	69.3
1910-1919	6,347,370	80.0°	62.4
1920-1929	4,295,510	73.0°	55.4
1930-1939	699,375	68.9°	42.5
1940-1949	856,608	67.1°	39.4

Based on U.S. Bureau of the Census, *Statistical History of the United States from Colonial Times to the Present* (Washington, 1966), 62.
° Between 1899 and 1918, the age group was 14 to 44 years. Between 1918 and 1940, the age group was 16 to 44 years. After 1940 and until 1944, the figures refer to those between 16 and 45. From 1945 to 1950 the age group was 16 to 44.

When the annual figures are averaged over ten years, immigration amounted to about one and one-quarter percent of the total population.[53] No other decade showed such a high average, and with one exception, 1900 to 1910, no other decade exceeded one percent.[54] The high proportion of men among these immigrants caused an increase in the foreign-born workers disproportionate to the number of arrivals. The trend was evident by 1870. In the decade that followed about one-sixth of the increase in the labor force was due to immigration.[55] In the 1880's immigration, with its large male contingent, accounted for one-third of the growth in the labor force and contributed to important changes for the total labor supply.[56]

Repatriation was even more heavily male than was immigration. Table IV shows the relationship for the years after 1908,

[53] *Ibid.*
[54] *Ibid.*
[55] Kuznets and Rubin, *Immigration and the Foreign Born*, 3.
[56] *Ibid.*

when records were first compiled by the United States Commissioner General of Immigration.

TABLE IV

PERCENTAGE OF MALES AMONG IMMIGRANTS TO
THE UNITED STATES AND EMIGRANT
ALIENS FROM THE UNITED STATES

Fiscal Year Ending June 30	Number of Males Per 100 Immigrants to U.S.	Number of Males Per 100 Emigrants From U.S.°
1908	64.8	86.8
1909	69.2	70.4
1910	70.7	76.5
1911	64.9	80.8
1912	63.2	82.8
1913	67.5	81.7
1914	65.6	79.8

Harry Jerome, *Migration and Business Cycles* (New York, 1926), 39-40.
° Includes alien males departing from the United States in steerage conditions.

The entire effect of repatriation on the labor force is underlined by a consideration of the total numbers involved. In 1908 the Immigration Commission reported that 395,073 emigrant aliens had left America in the preceding 12 months, a period of economic difficulty.[57] Nearly five out of six were males, and most of those who had held jobs had been working as laborers.[58] Table V shows the numbers engaged in some of the largest sectors.

The departure of hundreds of thousands of workers each year had important consequences for the economic life of the country although economists disagree over the exact nature of the effect. Harry Jerome, writing for the National Bureau of Economic Research, suggested that unlimited immigration during the upswing of a business cycle tended to furnish a surplus of workers and thus result in decreased production costs.[59] He wrote:

Our analysis would be incomplete if we failed to mention the not inconsiderable probability that the inflow of large numbers of new workers in the United States in times of prosperity has been a

[57] U.S. Commissioner General of Immigration, *Annual Report 1908* (Washington, 1908), 63.
[58] *Ibid.*, 79.
[59] Jerome, *Migration and Business Cycles*, 242.

TABLE V

OCCUPATIONS OF EMIGRANT ALIENS
FROM THE UNITED STATES
BETWEEN 1908 AND 1914

Fiscal Year Ending June 30	Professionals	Skilled Workers	Unskilled Workers
1908	2,218	37,801	279,669
1909	1,806	21,919	118,936
1910	3,280	21,574	89,396
1911	2,883	33,473	173,952
1912	3,056	35,898	209,279
1913	2,925	31,563	191,604
1914	2,873	35,160	176,642

U.S. Commissioner General of Immigration, *Annual Report* (Washington, 1908 to 1914), *passim*.

factor in increasing the intensity of boom periods and consequently the severity of a subsequent depression.[60]

Jerome concluded that reemigration sometimes mitigated the effects of cyclical variations in unemployment by withdrawing large numbers from the working force.[61] As a safety valve, however, the backward flow of persons functioned imperfectly. According to Jerome, time elapsed between the decreased need for labor and the departure of workers. In addition, two countries participated in the population exchange, and since both often underwent a similar business fluctuation at the same time, migration could not serve the interests of both of them.[62]

Simon Kuznets and Ernest Rubin expressed more certainty in their conclusions on the effect of emigration on the economic life of America. Also writing for the National Bureau of Economic Research, they noted that the limitations imposed by the quota legislation should have, if Jerome's analysis proved accurate, dampened the business downswing of the late 1920's and the effects of the depression.[63] They reasoned that the occurrence of the worst depression in America's history following immigration restriction did not support Jerome's findings.

---

[60] *Ibid.*

[61] *Ibid.*, 241.

[62] *Ibid.*, 242.

[63] Kuznets and Rubin, *Immigration and the Foreign Born*, 5-6.

Kuznets and Rubin reached the opposite conclusion. They suggested that the departure of large numbers of men from the labor supply soon after their arrival and the unrestricted entry of others in the setting which existed before 1921 might have furnished a valuable kind of safety valve.[64] They reasoned:

> Cyclical changes in inward and outward migration might serve to moderate the cycle, or at least its effects on unemployment of the native labor force. There is some evidence to show that most of the departures were from the pool of the recently arrived. A large proportion of the arrivals and departures were men, and of members of the labor force. Under conditions of free in-and outflow, one might therefore regard foreign labor supply as a sort of stabilizing reservoir.[65]

Economists have not limited themselves to considering the effects of reemigration on the labor force. Their work in that area indicates, however, the possible magnitude of its consequence. Not agreeing on the exact nature of the results of repatriation, economists have concurred in its importance.

Sociologists too have exhibited a great deal of interest in the experiences of persons who change countries. An examination of some of the literature in the field shows that the emphasis has centered on permanent immigration rather than on temporary settlement. A few sociologists have noted, however, that at a particular point in the process of adjusting to the adopted country, some immigrants reject the new home, or aspects of it, and return to the place they had left.

The term sociologists choose for the adjustment experience indicates their varied interpretations of the process. Robert E. Park, a pioneer in the study of the sociology of immigration, used the term "assimilation." He explained that it was the appropriate one since it implied a kind of physical change occurring when one group of people conformed to the ways of another. For Park, the entering group attempts unsuccessfully to become indistinguishable from the host society.[66] Although the immigrants themselves fail in the attempt, their children succeed. "Assimilation may be compared with grafting," Park wrote, "where the new tissue is not applied to

---

[64] *Ibid.*, 6.

[65] *Ibid.*

[66] Robert E. Park, *An Outline of the Principles of Sociology* (New York, 1939), 199.

the whole surface, but spots are grafted, and from these, the connecting tissues ramify."[67] Park's term continues to be the one most commonly used by sociologists including those who emphasize that immigration causes changes in both the new residents and the receiving culture.[68]

Other terms are commonly used to express the immigrants' experiences. S.N. Eisenstadt preferred the term "absorption" in discussing the change which took place when newcomers arrived in Israel to make their homes.[69] Other students of the subject have objected to the implications of both terms. They have insisted that "integration" is the more accurate description. William S. Bernard, Director of the Center for Migration Studies at Brooklyn College and one of the advocates of this term, wrote: "The fact of the matter is . . . . that the United States has not generally assimilated the newcomer or absorbed him; our immigrants and our so-called 'native Americans' have each integrated with the other."[70]

Whatever term is used, most sociologists agree that the impact of the host culture on the immigrant is accompanied by changes in that society which result from the newcomer's residence there. Aliens, for example, bring different views of how women should be treated and of what the family should mean; they add new words and new foods. Their neighbors adopt some of these changes, at the same time instructing them in their own ways.

In cases of repatriation, none of these terms seems appropriate. The individual who returned to his first country within five years of his arrival in the United States had not assimilated, or integrated or been absorbed. His inability or unwillingness to do so has been treated as his failure, and his contribution to an understanding of the process of changing cultures and countries has been largely ignored.

To the extent that students of the subject have acknowledged reemigration, they have disagreed over conditions in which it is most likely to occur. W. D. Borrie, a sociologist studying worldwide

---

[67] Robert E. Park and Herbert A. Miller, *Old World Traits Transplanted* (New York, 1921), 180.

[68] As representative examples, see: Milton M. Gordon, "Assimilation in America: Theory and Reality," *Daedalus*, XC (Spring 1961), 263-85; Nathan Glazer and Daniel Patrick Moynihan, *Beyond the Melting Pot* (Cambridge, 1963).

[69] S.N. Eisenstadt, *The Absorption of Immigrants* (Glencoe, 1955).

[70] William S. Bernard, "Integration of Immigrants in the United States," *International Migration Review*, I (Spring 1967), 23-33.

population shifts, summarized views expressed at the United Nations Educational, Scientific and Cultural Organization (UNESCO) Conference on the Integration of Immigrants held in Havana in 1956. The consensus was that a person who moved to a culture similar to the one he had left probably adjusted more successfully than an individual who chose a dissimilar country.[71] Borrie reported that several conditions affect the integration of an immigrant including his motivation for moving, proximity to his home country and the experiences of other members of his ethnic group.[72] Borrie noted that the similarity between the sending and receiving environments often, but not always, increases the chance that the move will be permanent.[73] He pointed to the ease with which Italians settled in Brazil. The Italian immigrant was psychologically better equipped, Borrie concluded, than a non-Latin for integrating himself in Brazilian society.[74]

Ilja Dijour, of the Hebrew Immigrant Aid Service (HIAS), attacked the assumption that people have fewer problems in immigrating to a similar society. Speaking before the Seminar on the Integration of Immigrants in 1960, he noted:

> If we would take a closer look at reemigration, we will find that the return of British from Australia, South Africa and Canada or Portuguese from Brazil, or of Spaniards and Italians from the rest of Latin America, is incomparably higher than the reemigration of say Japanese from Brazil, Slavic people from Australia and Canada, or others. There may be many reasons for this, but it should be possible to isolate the majority of cases where the main reason was an exaggerated expectation of finding no differences at all between the 'old' and the 'new' home in the case of the first group and a kind of psychological preparedness of the other group to finding everything different in the new country.[75]

Other sociologists have attempted to find the causes of immigrant satisfaction in the new country. Judith Shuval, a sociologist who has studied resettlement experiences in both Israel and the United States, suggested that the level of living an immigrant

---

[71] W.D. Borrie, *The Cultural Integration of Immigrants* (Paris, 1959), 99.

[72] *Ibid.*

[73] *Ibid.*

[74] *Ibid.*, 81.

[75] Ilja Dijour, "Seminar on the Integration of Immigrants," (Unpublished Report of the American Immigration and Citizenship Conference, New York, 1960), 6.

experienced before moving might affect his satisfaction with the new country.[76] In Israel, for instance, people who settled in temporary accommodations reacted in diverse ways. Shuval reported that those from a European background of more pleasant surroundings tended to be less satisfied with the transit camps than the non-Europeans. "This theory," Shuval concluded, "proposes that relative deprivation more or less sets the stage for the immigrant's initial reaction to Israel."[77]

Shuval's thesis was one of those tested by Jerold Heiss, the American sociologist, when he studied Italians in Australia. Heiss reasoned that if Shuval's findings for Israel held with Italians in Australia, then southern Italians would express less disappointment with their new country than the northern Italians since Sicilians and Neapolitans had come from less prosperous conditions than the northerners.[78] His findings were different from those of Shuval. He wrote:

> One cannot account for satisfaction merely on the basis of knowledge of amount of pre-emigration deprivation. The data show a complex relationship between satisfaction and length of residence, present status and mobility.[79]

In another article, Heiss reported his conclusions on the effect of living with one's own countrymen in the new environment.[80] In his sample group only a few Italians had separated themselves from their compatriots and lived among Australians. Their assimilation appeared, however, the easiest and most rapid of all groups examined.[81] Heiss did not conclude that he had isolated the most important factor in the integration of immigrants. He wrote: "If motivation to assimilate exists, one does not 'need' Australian friends."[82]

Heiss reported in other articles his attempts to account for the return home of some unhappy Italians and the expressed pleasure

---

[76] Judith T. Shuval, *Immigrants on the Threshold* (New York, 1963), 189.

[77] *Ibid.*

[78] Jerold Heiss, "Sources of Satisfaction and Assimilation among Italian Immigrants," *Human Relations*, XIX (May 1966), 165-177.

[79] *Ibid.*, 177.

[80] Jerold Heiss, "Factors Related to Immigrant Assimilation: The Early Post-Migration Situation," *Human Organization*, XXVI (Winter 1967), 265-72.

[81] *Ibid.*, 267.

[82] *Ibid.*, 268.

of others with their new country.[83] His work indicates the kinds of contributions that sociologists are making to the efforts of historians and economists to understand repatriation.

The literature of reemigration permits few undisputed conclusions. Relatively little information emerges concerning approximately 12 million persons, either their motivation for returning or the effects of their move. The following chapters report details of the Italian repatriation between 1900 and 1914. Official United States records exist only for the second half of that period, the years 1908 to 1914. During that time approximately 655,756 Italians left America.[84] Italian shipmasters' reports indicate that the movement in the preceding seven years had been similar in magnitude.[85] The migration of nearly 1.5 million persons is examined in the following pages in order to ascertain the kind of immigrant most likely to turn back, the response of the Italian government to the large number of returnees, and the effect which American residence caused in the lives of those who resettled in Italy.

---

[83] For a list of Heiss' articles, see Jerold Heiss, "Factors Related to Immigrant Assimilation: Pre-Migration Traits," *Social Forces*, XLVII (June 1969), 422-28.

[84] Willcox, *International Migrations*, I, 496.

[85] Foerster, *The Italian Emigration*, 30.

2

Extent and
Characteristics of
Italian Repatriation
from the
United States

THE MIGRATION of Italians between their country and the United States has undergone many changes since the first attempts were made to measure it. Italy contributed a small number of new settlers to North America before 1860, but by the end of the nineteenth century the peninsula had become an important source of population increase for the United States. Italian immigration reached its peak between 1900 and 1914, the same period in which repatriation attained its highest point. World War I subsequently dampened enthusiasm for travel in both directions across the Atlantic, and restrictive legislation of 1921 and 1924 applied an official brake.

The lack of available materials on Italian emigration and repatriation necessitates the use of reports from both countries involved in order to arrive at some conclusion on the extent and characteristics of the return movement. Information is particularly scarce on the early years. Before the unification of Italy in 1861 and for some years afterward no central agency existed to collect and classify information on the population drain from the peninsula. Students of emigration in that period had noted, however, that the exodus had already begun. Cesare Correnti, demographer and official observer, wrote for the *Annuario Statistico* of 1854-58:

> The number of Italians who are settled abroad or wandering there is large. Italian families have resided for centuries in the islands of Quarnero, in the Fiume, and in Dalmatia. Italian refugees, adventurers, tradesmen and doctors are scattered in all parts of the East. On the Algerian coast about 15,000 Italians have settled in the last ten years. The United States has received 10,000 emigrants, and three times that number of peddlers, laborers and tradesmen have located in Argentina, Uruguay, Brazil and other South American countries.[1]

French writers, noting the influx of Italians to their country before 1860, commented on the extent of that migration to other parts of the world. Jules Duval, one of the more productive nineteenth century French emigration scholars, reported that 7,185 Italians had entered the United States between 1819 and 1855.[2]

---

[1] Cesare Correnti, *Annuario Statistico Italiano, 1854-58* (Turin, 1858), 441.

[2] Jules Duval, *Histoire de l' Emigration Européenne, Asiatique et Afircaine au XIXe Siècle* (Paris, 1862), 157.

Leone Carpi, one of the first Italians to achieve a reputation in the study of modern population movements, observed that political motivations had caused departures of groups from Italy in 1815, 1821 and 1831.[3] Carpi's investigation focused, however, on the years following his country's unification, and his reports for the preceding period are incomplete since they are based on fragmentary accounts of local governments.

Since Italian records are unavailable for the years before 1860, American immigration statistics are the best indication of the extent of Italy's contribution to the United States. After 1820 captains of ships arriving in United States ports were required to submit lists of disembarking passengers, including the age, sex and occupation of each person, the country to which be "belonged," and the number that had not survived the journey.[4] These records are not entirely accurate since they do not include, for the early years, persons arriving in Pacific ports or crossing land boundaries to settle in the United States. Before 1867 alien passengers taken aboard were counted so that the total includes persons who died on the voyage. Foreigners stopping in the United States on their way to other countries were included between 1856 and 1867, a period in which they accounted for about one and one-half percent of the alien passenger arrivals.[5] Even with these limitations, reports indicate the relatively small number of Italians who emigrated to the United States before 1860. With the exception of 1833, which is so unusual as to arouse special suspicion as to its accuracy, no more than a few hundred Italians arrived in the United States in any one year before 1850. In 1820 Italians accounted for only 0.34 percent of the total arrivals and by 1860 they were 0.65 percent. At the time of the Civil War not one alien passenger in 100 gave a region of Italy as the place to which he "belonged."

Italian immigrants to the United States before 1860 tended to disperse themselves over the entire territory of the new country rather than congregate in eastern cities as later arrivals did. Andrew F. Rolle, American historian with a special interest in the western United States, wrote: "It is not possible to name all the Italians who settled along the lower Mississippi but it is known that their num-

---

[3] Leone Carpi, *Dell'Emigrazione Italiana all'Estero* (Florence, 1871), 58.

[4] U.S. Bureau of the Census, *Statistical History of the United States from Colonial Times to the Present* (Washington, 1966), 48.

[5] *Ibid.*, 49.

TABLE VI

IMMIGRATION TO THE UNITED STATES, 1820 TO 1860

Year	From All Countries	From Italy
1820	8,385	30
1821	9,127	63
1822	6,911	35
1823	6,354	33
1824	7,912	45
1825	10,199	75
1826	10,837	57
1827	18,875	35
1828	27,382	34
1829	22,520	23
1830	23,322	9
1831	22,633	28
1832	60,482	3
1833	58,640	1,699
1834	65,365	105
1835	45,374	60
1836	76,242	115
1837	79,340	36
1838	38,914	86
1839	68,069	84
1840	84,066	37
1841	80,289	179
1842	104,565	100
1843	52,496	117
1844	78,615	141
1845	114,371	137
1846	154,416	151
1847	234,968	164
1848	226,527	241
1849	297,024	209
1850	369,980	431
1851	379,466	447
1852	371,603	351
1853	368,645	555
1854	427,833	1,263
1855	200,877	1,052
1856	200,436	1,365
1857	251,306	1,007
1858	123,126	1,240
1859	121,282	932
1860	153,640	1,019

Based on U.S. Bureau of the Census, *Statistical History of the United States from Colonial Times to the Present* (Washington, 1966), 56-57.

bers increased steadily, especially after the European revolutions of 1848."[6]

Robert F. Foerster concluded that those who went to the United States before 1860 intended to remain. Foerster observed:

> Before 1860 the immigration appears to have been of persons who desired permanent settlement. That could be readily explained, without going further, by the difficulties of transportation. Chiefly the arrivals were north Italians, and they included, besides traders, many Lucchese vendors of plaster statuary and street musicians with monkeys—fantastic vanguard of the brawny army to follow.[7]

Italy contributed such a small part of the total American immigration in the years before 1860 that even a high percentage of repatriates would have had little significance for either country. The difficulty of the journey to the New World, its length and cost, as well as the choice of interior parts of the continent for settlement, suggest that most Italians who emigrated to the United States in that period became permanent Americans.

After 1860 a noticeable change took place in Italian immigration to America. No Italian government records on emigration exist for the years before 1875, but Leone Carpi's reports for the preceding years have semi-official status. Carpi noted the recent change in Italian migration to all parts of the world:

> It is only in the last 30 years that the great problem of emigration has begun to trouble Europe. Unfortunately, in relation to Italy, no one gave the matter serious attention so that acceptable statistics are missing even from states such as Piedmont in which emigration has been considerable.[8]

Carpi recommended that some central agency investigate the effect of migration because by 1869 his country was losing annually about six persons for every 1,000 inhabitants.[9] Carpi's examination of local records and of passenger lists of departing vessels showed that the Americas became increasingly popular with emigrating Italians in the 1860's. Between 1860 and 1869 a total of 94,186

---

[6] Andrew F. Rolle, *The Immigrant Upraised* (Norman, 1968), 58.
[7] Foerster, *The Italian Emigration*, 323.
[8] Carpi, *Dell'Emigrazione Italiana all'Estero*, 60.
[9] *Ibid.*, 116.

persons left Genoa for the western hemisphere.[10] Carpi's analysis of those going to the Americas showed that an increasing number came from southern Italy, a change which was noticeable within a two year span, 1866-68.

TABLE VII

ITALIAN EMIGRANTS TO THE AMERICAS
BY SECTION OF ORIGIN,
1866 TO 1868

Year		Number
1866	From the South	1,890
	From other regions	1,630
1867	From the South	6,783
	From other regions	5,689
1868	From the South	6,875
	From other regions	4,410

Based on Leone Carpi, *Dell' Emigrazione Italiana all' Estero* (Florence, 1871), 227.

Among those going to transoceanic ports between 1861 and 1869, the number of men was twice that of women. Carpi's examination of the occupations of those departing showed that the largest group (11,728) had worked in agriculture but had never owned land, while another sizeable number (8,497) had been skilled workers and tradesmen.[11] His findings show that all parts of the kingdom, except Sicily, were losing more population from rural than urban areas.

TABLE VIII

ITALIAN EMIGRANTS TO THE UNITED STATES
1873

From	Urban		Rural	
	Male	*Female*	*Male*	*Female*
Southern provinces (Mainland)	6,943	1,202	8,797	860
Piedmont and Liguria	5,666	1,894	26,231	6,264
Veneto	4,679	244	36,059	961
Sicily	1,132	242	271	124

Leone Carpi, *Delle Colonie e dell' Emigrazione d' Italiani all' Estero* (4 vols., Milan, 1874), III, 226.

[10] *Ibid.*, 224.
[11] Capri, *Dell' Emigrazione Italiana all' Estero*, 224.

Giovanni Florenzano, a contemporary compatriot of Carpi's and also a student of migration, examined 16 provinces in the Naples area for an 18-month period including 1872 and the first half of 1873.[12] His work emphasized the extent of emigration to America and attempted to fill what he considered to be a lamentable gap in information on those leaving Italy. Florenzano noted that no statistical material existed on emigration in any publication of his government at the time he was writing.[13]

The formation of the *Direzione Generale della Statistica* in 1876 manifested the first official cognizance of the importance of Italian departures and, indirectly, of the impermanent nature of much of the emigration. From that year until 1904 the basis of the information published by the *Direzione Generale della Statistica* was the *nulla osta*, or exit permit, which local authorities granted to persons in order that they might apply for passports.[14] When requesting the *nulla osta*, each individual was asked whether he planned to leave Italy temporarily or permanently. Obvious problems existed to hinder the use of these documents as actual counts of the numbers leaving and of the length of their absence. Many of the applicants did not know what they intended to do. Others did not understand the question, and some may have had reasons for hiding their intentions. Unfortunately Italy's physical make-up allowed for no more accurate an enumeration. The *Commissariato Generale dell' Emigrazione*, established in 1901 to assist the *Direzione Generale* in gathering information, listed some of its problems:

> The phenomenon of emigration is difficult to measure in a country such as Italy which has a coastline of 6000 kilometers with numerous mountain passes across which it is easy to leave the country. In such conditions, since it was not possible to count emigrants at the exit place, it was necessary to resort to local offices of the town, asking periodically how many people had requested documents to emigrate. The principal object of this inquiry was the *nulla osta* which had to be given by the town officials before a passport could be obtained from government authorities. Also there was some inquiry among the townspeople as

---

[12] Giovanni Florenzano, *Della Emigrazione Italiana in America* (Naples, 1874).

[13] *Ibid.*, 121.

[14] Commissariato Generale dell'Emigrazione, *L'Emigrazione Italiana* (Rome, 1925), 11.

to whether they had any personal knowledge of individuals who had left.[15]

Although not entirely accurate because of the way in which they were compiled, the reports of the *Direzione Generale della Statistica* for the years 1876-1899 indicate that greater numbers left Italy each year and that the proportion going to the United States continued to increase.

TABLE IX

ITALIAN EMIGRATION, 1876-1899
ACCORDING TO OFFICIAL ITALIAN RECORDS

Year	Total Italians Leaving°	Per 100,000 Inhabitants°°	To The United States°
1876	108,771	395	1,441°°°
1877	99,213	358	976°°°
1878	96,268	345	1,993°°°
1879	119,831	428	3,114
1880	119,901	425	5,711
1881	135,832	479	11,482
1882	161,562	565	18,593
1883	169,101	588	21,256
1884	147,017	507	10,582
1885	157,193	538	12,485
1886	167,829	571	26,920
1887	215,665	728	37,221
1888	290,736	975	32,945
1889	218,412	727	25,434
1890	215,854	718	47,952
1891	293,631	964	44,359
1892	223,667	729	42,953
1893	246,751	799	49,765
1894	225,323	725	31,668
1895	293,181	937	37,851
1896	307,482	976	53,486
1897	299,855	946	47,000
1898	283,715	889	56,375
1899	308,339	960	63,156

° Based on Istituto Centrale di Statistica, *Sommario di Statistiche Storiche Italiane: 1861-1955* (Rome, 1958), 65-66.
°° Based on Commissariato Generale dell'Emigrazione, *L'Emigrazione Italiana* (Rome, 1925), 34ff.
°°° Includes persons going to Canada.

[15] *Ibid.*

By the end of the century, nearly one person departed for every 100 who remained, and approximately one-fifth of the emigrants indicated the United States as their destination. American reports, compiled by the Department of State before 1870, by the Bureau of Statistics in the Treasury Department for 1870-1895 and by the Office of Immigration after 1895, also show that the United States had become popular with Italian emigrants by 1900.

Not all regions lost the same percentage of their migration to the United States. An examination of three two-year periods within the last quarter of the nineteenth century supports the observation Carpi made in the 1860's that a larger part of the emigration to America came from southern Italy. The trend developed more clearly as the years passed. Sicily, for example, sent only five percent of its emigrants to the United States in 1876-78; by 1884-86 the number rose to more than 60 percent; and with the passage of another decade the corresponding figure was 64 percent.

Italy contributed large numbers to North America by the turn of the century, but it was from the southern regions that the greater part came. In the years 1894-96, Abruzzi, Molise, Campania, Basilicata, Apulia and Sicily all contributed more than one-third of their emigrants to the United States; and Calabria sent one-fifth.

The port inspectors who concluded that Italians departing for the Americas would settle permanently abroad, as their countrymen had done before 1860, soon learned of their error. Available information indicated well before 1900 that many Italian emigrants chose to return to the land of their birth. Both Carpi and Florenzano observed that emigrants after 1860 often went back to Italy following a period of residence abroad. Carpi wrote:

> Several persons have noted that since 1866 thousands of Italians go to search work abroad, then come back within a year or two bringing with them a small amount of savings along with some bad habits.[16]

Florenzano noted:

> Our statistics committee affirms that our emigrants carry their mother country in their hearts and maintain a political tie with it, and that they return as soon as they have put together a small

---

[16] Leone Carpi, *Delle Colonie e dell'Emigrazione d'Italiani all'Estero* (4 vols., Milan, 1874), I, 75.

TABLE X

IMMIGRATION TO THE UNITED STATES, 1861-1899

Year	Total Immigration	From Italy
1861	91,918	811
1862	91,985	566
1863	176,282	547
1864	193,418	600
1865	248,120	924
1866	318,568	1,382
1867	315,722	1,624
1868	138,840	891
1869	352,768	1,489
1870	387,203	2,891
1871	321,350	2,816
1872	404,806	4,190
1873	459,803	8,757
1874	313,339	7,666
1875	227,498	3,631
1876	169,986	3,015
1877	141,857	3,195
1878	138,469	4,344
1879	177,826	5,791
1880	457,257	12,354
1881	669,431	15,401
1882	788,992	32,159
1883	603,322	31,792
1884	518,592	16,510
1885	395,346	13,642
1886	334,203	21,315
1887	490,109	47,622
1888	546,889	51,558
1889	444,427	25,307
1890	455,302	52,003
1891	560,319	76,055
1892	579,663	61,631
1893	439,730	72,145
1894	285,631	42,977
1895	258,536	35,427
1896	343,267	68,060
1897	230,832	59,431
1898	229,299	58,613
1899	311,715	77,419

Based on U.S. Bureau of the Census, *Statistical History of the United States from Colonial Times to the Present* (Washington, 1966), 56-57.

TABLE XI

ITALIANS TO THE UNITED STATES
BY REGION OF ORIGIN, 1876-1896°

Region	1876-78	1884-86	1894-96
Piedmont	114	745	606
	0.42%	2.62%	2.30%
Liguria	320	706	745
	8.82%	12.05%	17.64%
Lombardy	320	372	976
	8.82%	1.87%	5.01%
Veneto	33	179	492
	0.10%	0.40%	0.48%
Emilia	25	189	706
	0.73%	3.78%	6.06%
Tuscany	129	283	996
	2.00%	2.69%	7.81%
Marches	3	25	232
	1.06%	1.21%	3.47%
Umbria	—	12	49
	—	28.69%	12.77%
Lazio	1	2	109
	1.59%	11.11%	12.40%
Abruzzi and			
Molise	50	2,811	5,288
	6.33%	38.85%	33.01%
Campania	476	3,957	14,557
	13.57%	30.80%	46.86%
Basilicata	78	3,486	3,314
	5.04%	43.35%	34.70%
Apulia	9	171	1,590
	2.25%	22.02%	34.62%
Calabria	34	1,575	3,726
	2.34%	18.68%	22.05%
Sicily	50	1,791	7,613
	4.90%	60.52%	63.67%
Sardinia	1	—	3
	3.13%	—	0.32%
Italy	1,470	16,662	41,002
	1.45%	10.59%	14.89%

Based on Luigi Rossi, *Relazione sui Servizi dell'Emigrazione per l'Anno 1909-1910* (Rome, 1910), 478.
° Whole number in each column represents total emigration to the United States from that region. Percentage refers to portion of total emigration from the region which was directed toward the United States.

ILLUSTRATION I

ITALIAN EMIGRANTS TO THE UNITED STATES BY ORIGIN IN ITALY: 1894-1896

PERCENTAGE OF TOTAL
EMIGRATION DIRECTED
TOWARD THE U.S.

LESS THAN 5%

BETWEEN 5 AND 15%

BETWEEN 16 AND 30%

OVER 30%

Based on Luigi Rossi, *Relazione sui Servizi dell'Emigrazione per l'Anno, 1909-1910* (Rome, 1910), 476.

nestegg. In this respect, they are different from the English, Irish and Germans who go to America to become citizens.[17]

Florenzano's estimate of the number of repatriates was lower than those of others he cited. In his opinion, about one-ninth returned of those who emigrated to America from the Naples vicinity.[18] Different areas within the section studied had varying return rates. Salerno, for example, reported 4,539 emigrants in 1872 and 900 repatriates, while Cosenza noted 2,902 leaving and 253 returning.[19] This meant that Salerno got one-fifth of its population loss back that year while Cosenza regained only one-twelfth of its emigrants.

Both Carpi and Florenzano indicated that the return movement was increasing, but they lacked the means to measure it. The *Direzione Generale della Statistica* took official notice of the repatriation from the Americas in 1884 when it began to require that captains of ships arriving in Italy supply the Ministry of Marine with a list of passengers, the class in which they had traveled and the country from which third class passengers had sailed.[20] The nationality of the passengers was not noted before 1902, but evidence suggests that few non-Italians chose to travel third-class to Italy.[21] The number of arrivals in the least expensive accommodations did not necessarily include all Italians repatriating; some persons returning to reside in Italy may have sailed to non-Italian ports and then proceeded by train. Others may have returned in first or second class accommodations. Evidence suggests, however, that few repatriates chose the better class journey and that, in general, the number of persons arriving in third class is a good indication of the extent of Italian repatriation each year. About one in six of those returning in 1884 came from the United States, but by 1899 that country was the embarcation point for nearly one in two.

In spite of the large number recorded as returning, the Italian government took little official notice, and local offices continued until 1904 to classify as permanent emigrants those persons who specified a transoceanic port as their destination.[22]

---

[17] Florenzano, *Della Emigrazione Italiana in America*, 289.
[18] *Ibid.*, 291.
[19] *Ibid.*
[20] Direzione Generale della Statistica, *Statistica della Emigrazione Italiana, 1896/97* (Rome, 1898), xx.
[21] *Ibid.*
[22] Commissariato Generale dell'Emigrazione, *L'Emigrazione Italiana*, 13.

TABLE XII

PASSENGERS ARRIVING IN ITALIAN PORTS
IN THIRD CLASS ACCOMMODATIONS,
1884-1899

Year	From United States	Total
1884	2,667	12,908
1885	n.a.	n.a.
1886	n.a.	n.a.
1887	3,000	18,039
1888	6,072	27,281
1889	4,734	33,576
1890	2,881	45,880
1891	10,170	60,710
1892	12,695	51,699
1893	22,912	53,634
1894	26,845	55,221
1895	17,039	53,962
1896	20,885	58,607
1897	22,292	63,893
1898	24,735	71,687
1899	31,289	69,441

Direzione Generale della Statistica, *Statistica della Emigrazione Italiana, 1896/7* to *1914/5* (Rome, 1896-1915), *passim.*

The greatest population movement between the United States and Italy occurred in the period 1900 to 1914. Statistics of both countries concur that mass emigration and repatriation took place in these years. Italian records indicate that more than three million nationals left for the United States during a time when the total population ranged between 32 and 36 million.[23] Official American enumeration showed that Italy had contributed less than five percent of the foreign born persons residing in the United States as the time of the 1900 census, but the figure had risen to nearly ten percent by 1910.[24] Table XIII gives the official statistics of the *Direzione Generale della Statistica* for emigrants each year between 1900 and 1914 and shows the number who indicated the United States as their destination. In 1905, 1906, 1907, 1912 and 1913 more

[23] Istituto Centrale di Statistica, *Sommario di Statistiche Storiche Italiane: 1861-1955* (Rome, 1958), 39.
[24] U.S. Bureau of the Census, *Thirteenth Census of the United States Taken in the Year 1910: Abstract of the Census* (Washington, 1913), 188.

than two Italians left for each 100 then residing in that country and more than one-third of those leaving headed for the United States.

TABLE XIII

ITALIAN EMIGRATION, 1900 TO 1914

Year	Total Emigration°	Per 100,000 Inhabitants°°	To The U.S.°
1900	352,782	1,091	87,714
1901	533,245	1,638	121,139
1902	531,509	1,623	193,772
1903	507,976	1,543	197,855
1904	471,191	1,422	168,789
1905	726,331	2,177	316,797
1906	787,977	2,349	358,569
1907	704,675	2,086	298,124
1908	486,674	1,426	131,501
1909	625,637	1,818	280,351
1910	651,475	1,874	262,554
1911	533,844	1,539	191,087
1912	711,446	2,031	267,637
1913	872,598	2,464	376,776
1914	479,152	1,336	167,481

° Based on Istituto Centrale di Statistica, *Sommario di Statistiche Storiche Italiane: 1861-1955* (Rome, 1958), 65-66.
°° Based on Commissariato Generale dell'Emigrazione, *L'Emigrazione Italiana* (Rome, 1925), 34ff.

After 1902 the *Commissariato Generale dell'Emigrazione* compiled its own statistics on the number leaving Italy each year. The *Commissariato* based its conclusions on ship captains' reports of the number of passengers in third class traveling to transoceanic ports.[25] The total numbers of Italians bound for the United States between 1902 and 1912, as reported by the *Direzione Generale della Statistica*, the *Commissariato dell'Emigrazione* and the United States Immigration Office, do not vary greatly. The differences shown in Table XIV, result in part from the methods of gathering the information and from the use of fiscal year rather than calendar by American authorities.

Official Italian bulletins noted that emigration increased in the early years of the twentieth century:

---

[25] Commissariato Generale dell'Emigrazione, *L'Emigrazione Italiana*, 27.

TABLE XIV

COMPARISON OF THREE SETS OF
STATISTICS ON ITALIAN EMIGRATION TO
THE UNITED STATES, 1902-1906

Year	Direzione Generale	Commissariato Dell'Emigrazione	United States Immigration Office
1902	193,772	191,767	180,535
1903	197,855	214,157	233,546
1904	168,789	142,327	196,028
1905	316,797	252,521	226,320
1906	358,659	929,070	286,814
TOTAL	1,235,872	1,092,842	1,123,243

Commissariato dell'Emigrazione, *Bollettino dell'Emigrazione*, no. 11 (1907), 28.

After 1901 the exodus of Italian workers intensified rapidly reaching in the period, 1901-1913, an annual average of 626,000 emigrants . . . . The number designating transoceanic ports as their destination kept increasing.[26]

The United States took an ever larger part of the westward migration, a change also recorded by Italian officials:

Until 1899 emigration to the United States was overshadowed by that to Brazil, and, in some periods, by that to Argentina . . . . In the period 1900-1914 we note that the United States got two-thirds of all Italian emigrants to the Americas.[27]

Southern Italians continued to predominate among those going to the United States after 1900. Table XV shows the percentages of those leaving each region who indicated that they intended to settle in the United States. The entire peninsula sent to North America more than 40 percent of its emigrants, but for Lazio, Calabria and Sicily, the figure often exceeded 60 percent.

The passenger lists of ships arriving in Italy between 1900 and 1914 indicate the temporary nature of much of the emigration to America. The same limitations apply to the use of these reports as an indication of the number of repatriates in the period 1900 to

---

[26] Commissariato Generale dell'Emigrazione, *L'Emigrazione Italiana*, 27.

[27] *Ibid.*, 29.

TABLE XV

ITALIANS TO THE UNITED STATES
BY ORIGIN, 1906-1909°

Region	1904-6	1907	1908	1909
Piedmont	11,896	13,698	6,005	8,491
	17.70%	21.66%	10.82%	15.08%
Liguria	2,602	2,965	1,329	1,716
	33.14%	34.99%	20.56%	22.53%
Lombardy	5,598	6,790	2,992	4,603
	9.82%	11.14%	5.63%	9.17%
Veneto	5,077	6,491	3,985	4,694
	4.77%	6.11%	4.46%	5.62%
Emilia	6,384	7,171	3,799	5,538
	17.23%	17.45%	10.85%	18.17%
Tuscany	7,843	10,159	4,457	8,005
	24.77%	27.13%	15.21%	25.76%
Marches	6,100	6,542	3,000	6,172
	21.49%	26.61%	15.66%	26.91%
Umbria	1,952	3,471	1,086	2,773
	18.67%	22.21%	10.64%	25.98%
Lazio	10,466	13,491	5,598	14,603
	78.93%	70.73%	66.47%	86.2%
Abruzzi and Molise	33,978	33,279	14,902	39,440
	68.36%	65.90%	51.08%	73.80%
Campania	62,372	59,392	25,721	53,511
	83.18%	78.00%	69.27%	78.61%
Basilicata	9,604	9,936	4,394	8,354
	61.35%	65.85%	43.40%	60.2%
Apulia	15,552	20,446	8,662	17,069
	67.66%	68.81%	53.27%	62.09%
Calabria	33,180	27,510	13,752	32,247
	64.28%	58.25%	45.01%	61.40%
Sicily	68,067	75,594	31,215	72,429
	71.78%	77.44%	61.87%	76.38%
Sardinia	714	1,189	644	706
	15.26%	10.20%	9.79%	12.54%
Italy	281,385	298,124	131,501	280,351
	41.77%	42.31%	27.02%	44.81%

Based on Luigi Rossi, *Relazione sui Servizi dell'Emigrazione per l'Anno 1909-1910* (Rome, 1910), 478.
° Whole number in each column represents total emigration to the United States from that region. Percentage refers to portion of total emigration from the region which was directed toward the United States.

1914 as were noted above for the earlier years. However, Table XVI shows that larger numbers returned to Italy each year from transoceanic ports and that increasing numbers of these repatriates came from the United States. If no duplication occurred because of repeated journeys by the same individual, more than one and one-half million Italians returned to their home country between 1900 and 1914 after a period of temporary residence in the United States. Nearly one in 20 of the inhabitants of the peninsula deserved the name "*Americano*" as those who returned were called.

TABLE XVI

PASSENGERS ARRIVING IN ITALIAN PORTS
IN THIRD CLASS ACCOMMODATIONS, 1900-1914

Year	Total	From United States
1900	80,570	31,966
1901	77,567	24,678
1902	92,707	52,216
1903	120,645	78,233
1904	168,379	129,231
1905	96,156	68,821
1906	174,949	121,620
1907	248,979	177,278
1908	304,675	244,718
1909	134,207	73,803
1910	161,148	106,705
1911	218,998	156,205
1912	182,990	129,649
1913	188,978	122,589
1914	219,178	156,274

Direzione Generale della Statistica, *Statistica della Emigrazione Italiana, 1900/01* to *1914/15* (Rome, 1900 to 1915), *passim*.

In addition to the debarcation statistics, another basis existed after 1901 for estimating the number of repatriates. According to the law of September 21, 1901, all Italians returning from abroad after emigrating were required to go within one month of their arrival to the registry of the town where they were currently living in order to announce their presence and be reinstated on the list of local residents.[28] It is not clear that the individual involved perceived any special benefit for himself in complying with this

---

[28] *Ibid.*, 23.

law, even if he had been aware of its existence; and many of those returning seem to have ignored it. An examination of the statistics on reinstatements supports the conclusion that some parts of Italy had a much higher rate of repatriation than others. The report did not include the country of temporary residence, and any conclusion from these figures as to the number of *Americani* from the United States is unwarranted. Table XVII supports the observation of the *Direzione Generale della Statistica* that a sizeable percentage of Italian nationals returned between 1900 and 1914, much as their countrymen had emigrated temporarily in the latter part of the nineteenth century.

TABLE XVII

PERCENTAGE OF EMIGRANTS FROM EACH REGION
APPLYING TO LOCAL REGISTRIES FOR
REINSTATMENT AFTER RESIDENCE ABROAD

Region	1906-8	1909-10	1910-11
Piedmont	23	26	16
Liguria	47	42	37
Lombardy	32	24	18
Veneto	23	18	11
Emilia	28	24	13
Tuscany	33	23	15
Marches	18	17	9
Umbria	25	11	12
Lazio	18	19	8
Abruzzi	21	18	12
Campania	27	17	15
Apulia	29	27	13
Basilicata	32	27	20
Calabria	18	15	10
Sicily	22	24	11
Sardinia	4	7	6
Italy	24	21	13

Direzione Generale della Statistica, *Statistica della Emigrazione Italiana, 1908/9* (Rome, 1910), xxiv.

After the *Direzione Generale della Statistica* reported that more than 168,000 nationals had disembarked in home ports in 1904, the Italian government ordered an extensive investigation of those returning the following two years. The results of this study, published in separate works by Alberto Beneduce and Luigi Rossi, provide additional information on the contribution of the United States to the return migration.[29]

That many Italians had been repatriating each year from North America had been known for some time but the study of the returnees in 1905-6 showed that those coming from the United States had somewhat different characteristics than those leaving other parts of the Americas. Beneduce, noted, for example, that women constituted about one in ten (10.7% in 1905 and 13.3% in 1906) of those Italians returning from the United States while more than half of those leaving Brazil were female.[30] The same author observed that the United States was unique among countries of the western hemisphere for the great number of single Italians who departed in 1905-6. More than three-fourths of those leaving the United States traveled alone rather than with families while about one-fourth of those departing from Brazil were single individuals.[31]

An analysis of the months chosen for travel in both directions across the Atlantic showed that immigration to the United States reached its peak in March, April and May, three months in which nearly half of the year's total arrived.[32] The period of greatest repatriation, however, occurred between October and December when more than half of the yearly total of returnees reached home.[33] Because of the seasonal nature of the repatriation movement, as well as the predominance of single men and the absence of family groups among those involved, Beneduce concluded that the United States received Italy's temporary emigration composed principally of workers.[34] His materials did not include a breakdown of the occupations of the returnees so that his conclusion, in this respect, was impressionistic, but it gained support from the findings of the United States Immigration Commission which published its own information on the occupations of aliens departing after 1908.

Beneduce's analysis of the ages of the repatriating workers

---

[29] Luigi Rossi, *Relazione sui Servizi dell'Emigrazione per l'Anno 1909-1910* (Rome, 1910), and Alberto Beneduce, "Saggio di Statistica dei Rimpatriati dalle Americhe" in Commissariato Generale dell'Emigrazione, *Bollettino dell'Emigrazione*, no. 11 (1911), 1-103.

[30] Beneduce, "Saggio di Statistica dei Rimpatriati," 33.

[31] *Ibid.*, 39.

[32] *Ibid.*, 20.

[33] *Ibid.*, 25.

[34] *Ibid.*, 33.

TABLE XVIII

**ITALIAN EMIGRANT ALIENS FROM THE UNITED
STATES BETWEEN 1908 AND 1914:
BY OCCUPATION**

	1908°	1909°	1910°	1911°
North Italians°°				
Professional	100	189	270	438
Skilled	3,726	2,904	2,735	4,902
Farm laborers	1,101	291	424	2,802
Farmers	122	3,833	179	538
Laborers	11,969	9,326	6,275	12,524
South Italians				
Professional	189	294	173	495
Skilled	5,807	10,524	2,766	16,960
Farm laborers	524	2,147	540	53,988
Farmers	367	51,961	307	825
Laborers	124,914	58,155	29,777	32,370

	1912°	1913°	1914°
North Italians°°			
Professional	97	81	77
Skilled	2,531	1,953	2,614
Farm Laborers	56	23	9
Farmers	117	89	132
Laborers	7,699	6,632	7,164
South Italians			
Professional	202	132	131
Skilled	4,691	3,998	3,982
Farm Laborers	679	257	27
Farmers	225	122	131
Laborers	81,102	64,118	58,517

U.S. Commissioner General of Immigration, *Annual Report* (Washington, 1908 to 1914), *passim.*
° Fiscal Year ending June 30.
°° In reports of the U.S. Commissioner General of Immigration, northern Italians are persons from Piedmont, Lombardy, Emilia and Veneto. All other Italians are considered southerners.

revealed that they brought a high potential for productivity. More than one-third of the men returning to Italy from the United States in 1905-6 reported ages between 26 and 35, one-fifth between 36 and 45 and another fifth between 16 and 25.

Beneduce concluded that more than 75 percent of the returning group were in the most productive years (16 to 45) at a

TABLE XIX

ITALIANS RETURNING FROM THE UNITED STATES
IN 1905-1906: BY AGE AND SEX

	Less than 1 year	1-15 Years	16-25 Years	26-35 Years	36-45 Years
1905					
Male	1,035	2,973	12,507	21,305	11,972
Female	728	1,894	1,377	1,972	757
1906					
Male	1,262	3,285	16,268	30,148	15,699
Female	866	2,138	1,502	2,191	876

	46-55 Years	56-65 Years	Over 65 Years	Age Unknown
1905				
Male	3,767	933	173	5,840
Female	402	195	54	676
1906				
Male	4,269	982	198	15,762
Female	419	235	58	1,120

Based on Alberto Beneduce, "Saggio di Statistica dei Rimpatriati dalle Americhe" in Commissariato Generale dell'Emigrazione, *Bollettino dell'Emigrazione*, no. 11 (1911), 36.

time when the resident population of Italy had only 41.3 percent of its number in the same age span.[35] Only 3.7 percent of the repatriates reported that they were over 56 years of age, and these were mostly women returning to southern Italy to apply for pensions of workers in America.[36]

Luigi Rossi, a member of the Council on Emigration, agreed with Beneduce that the ages of the returnees helped explain the nature of the two-directional migration and its effect on Italy. Rossi wrote:

The distribution of repatriates by age seems to show the periodic character of a great part of our transoceanic emigration. The tendency is for that emigration to become a back and forth flow of labor in which the same people participate a number of times and while the group of old men diminishes, new groups reinforce the

---

[35] Beneduce, "Saggio di Statistica dei Rimpatriati," 33.
[36] *Ibid.*

emigrating current so that it succeeds in taking away the productive energy of the country.[37]

Both Beneduce and Rossi agreed that the same people had made the transoceanic journey many times but available American statistics do not support this conclusion. United States immigration officials inquired of each alien passenger who arrived in the United States between 1899 and 1910 if he had been in the country previously. After 1908 only those who indicated that they intended to settle were questioned. In the 12 years, 1899 to 1910, about one in six of the arriving Italians replied that he had been in the United States earlier. Among northern Italians, 15.2 percent reported a previous journey and among southern Italians the figure was 13.7 percent.[38] If these statistics are accurate, Rossi and Beneduce seem to have exaggerated the repeated participation of the same individuals in the backward and forward migration.

If the same individual made repeated trips to the United States, evidence from both countries suggests that each period of residence in the adopted country was of substantial duration. Rossi noted that the average stay in the United States was about five years, considerably longer than the time most Italian emigrants stayed in South America before returning to the country of their birth.[39] Rossi's conclusion is supported by American statistics available for the years after 1908.[40]

Italian emigrants to the United States may have remained slightly longer than those who resided temporarily in other parts of the New World but they did not exhibit greater wealth in their choice of accommodations for the return voyage. Table XX shows, for example, that more than 96 percent of those Italians leaving the United States traveled in third class. The corresponding figure for Central America was 73 percent in 1905 and 74 percent in 1906.

The 1905-6 study indicated once again how many of the repatriates went to southern Italy. Only about one-half of those returning from the United States indicated their destination, but Beneduce's examination of this group of respondents showed the heavy concentration of repatriates in the *Mezzogiorno*.

[37] Rossi, *Relazione sui Servizi dell'Emigrazione*, 35.

[38] U.S. Immigration Commission, 1907-1910, *Report of the Immigration Commission* (41 vols., Washington, 1911), III, 359.

[39] Rossi, *Relazione sui Servizi dell'Emigrazione*, 40.

[40] U.S. Commissioner General of Immigration, *Annual Report* (Washington, 1908 to 1914), *passim*.

ILLUSTRATION II

ITALIAN REPATRIATES FROM THE UNITED STATES
IN 1905-1906: BY DESTINATION IN ITALY

Based on Alberto Beneduce, "Saggio di Statistica dei Rimpatriati dalle Americhe"
in Commissariato Generale dell'Emigrazione, *Bollettino dell'Emigrazione*, no. 11
(1911), 96.

TABLE XX

ITALIANS ARRIVING IN ITALIAN PORTS IN 1906
BY CLASS OF VOYAGE

Departing From	1st and 2nd Class		3rd Class	
	Number	% of Total	Number	% of Total
United States	4,042	4.0	97,278	96.0
Brazil	808	4.5	17,236	95.5
Plata	3,803	11.1	30,393	88.9
Central America	317	27.0	859	73.0

Based on Alberto Beneduce, "Saggio di Statistica dei Rimpatriati dalle Americhe" in Commissariato Generale dell'Emigrazione, *Bollettino dell'Emigrazione*, no. 11 (1911), 36.

TABLE XXI

ITALIAN REPATRIATES FROM THE UNITED STATES
IN 1905-1906: BY SEX AND DESTINATION IN ITALY

	1905			1906		
	men	women	total	men	women	total
Piedmont	327	144	471	297	117	414
Liguria	787	269	1,056	555	201	756
Lombardy	465	137	602	448	137	585
Veneto	315	62	377	214	27	241
Emilia	353	139	492	294	100	394
Tuscany	588	152	740	609	99	708
Marches	527	40	567	636	35	671
Umbria	110	12	122	277	28	305
Lazio	1,059	55	1,114	2,382	70	2,452
Abruzzi and Molise	4,853	371	5,224	6,472	449	6,921
Campania	14,368	2,050	16,418	14,727	1,819	16,546
Puglia	1,205	113	1,318	2,007	130	2,137
Basilicata	1,079	123	1,202	1,523	168	1,691
Calabria	4,655	364	5,019	7,151	466	7,617
Sicily	5,694	1,024	6,718	10,268	1,676	11,944
Sardinia	9	—	9	28	3	31
Total	36,394	5,055	41,449	47,888	5,525	53,413
Without Indication	24,066	3,000	27,066	39,985	3,880	43,865
TOTAL	60,460	8,055	68,515	87,873	9,405	97,278

Based on Alberto Beneduce, "Saggio di Statistica dei Rimpatriati dalle Americhe" in Commissariato Generale dell'Emigrazione, *Bollettino dell'Emigrazione*, no. 11 (1911), 96.

Beneduce reported how many men and women reemigrated to each region in 1905-6. Table XXI indicates the high proportion of males among the returnees.

Rossi's report concurred that 75 to 90 percent of those who renewed their residence in Sicily, Campania, Abruzzi, Lazio and Apulia had come from the United States.[41] He concluded that the *Mezzogiorno* got back a higher percentage of its total emigration than did other sections of the country:

From the United States, it is calculated (without making allowances for those who travel back and forth more than once)

TABLE XXII

ITALIAN REPATRIATES FROM THE UNITED STATES IN 1905-1906 COMPARED TO EMIGRANTS IN 1901-1902 AND 1905-1906: BY REGION

Region	Number returned in 1905-6	Per 100 emigrants in 1901-2	Per 100 emigrants in 1905-6
Piedmont	1,530	16.4	5.6
Liguria	3,128	97.3	57.7
Lombardy	2,063	54.4	16.2
Veneto	1,061	35.6	8.8
N. Italy	7,782	40.0	13.5
Emilia	1,535	34.7	10.3
Tuscany	2,504	28.7	14.9
Marches	2,165	40.8	14.0
Umbria	753	62.5	15.0
Lazio	6,308	92.9	22.9
Central Italy	13,265	50.2	16.6
Abruzzi and Molise	21,240	39.8	25.7
Campania	57,277	62.8	38.9
Apulia	6,070	57.0	15.7
Basilicata	5,061	26.2	23.2
Calabria	22,169	75.9	28.5
Sicily	32,857	50.3	19.6
Sardinia	72	248.3	3.5
Southern Italy and islands	144,746	53.8	26.9
TOTAL	165,793	52.7	24.5

Alberto Beneduce, "Saggio di Statistica dei Rimpatriati dalle Americhe" in Commissariato Generale dell'Emigrazione, *Bollettino dell'Emigrazione*, no. 11 (1911), 96.

---

[41] Rossi, *Relazione sui Servizi dell'Emigrazione*, 38.

that 52 percent return; 53.8 percent of the southern Italians, 50.2 percent of those from central Italy and 40 percent of the northern Italians. Calabria receives 75.9 percent of its emigrants to the United States back; Campania, Apulia and Sicily regain more than half of theirs and Basilicata reclaims 26.2 percent of its emigrants.[42]

Rossi's conclusions support those of Beneduce who compared the number returning to each region in 1905-1906 with the number who had left the same area in 1901-1902 and in 1905-1906. He was thus able to ascertain how much of the population loss to the United States which each region had sustained in 1901-1902 was recovered in the two-year period at the end of the average temporary residence in America. Beneduce's figures show the extent to which returnees in 1905-06 compensated for current population losses.

Between 1900 and 1914 the Italian government acquired statistical basis for concluding that large numbers of its most able workers left each year for the United States and returned after an average stay of five years. The families of hundreds of thousands of young men remained in Italy while their husbands, sons and fathers worked in America. With this information on the extent and characteristics of the temporary emigration from the peninsula, the Italian government could augment or restrain the movement depending on the benefits or difficulties thought to result from it.

---

[42] *Ibid.*

3

Reaction of the
Italian Government to
Repatriation From
the United States
Between 1902 and
1914 as Reported
in the *Bollettino
Dell'Emigrazione*

THE PASSAGE of the Emigration Act of January 31, 1901, signified cognizance on the part of the Italian government of the need to regulate and report on migration from its borders. That legislation provided for the establishment of a *Commissariato dell' Emigrazione*, a technical organ, which was to operate under the jurisdiction of a Council on Emigration within the Ministry of Foreign Affairs. The Council included a delegate from the ministries of Foreign Affairs, Internal Affairs, Treasury, Marine, Public Instruction and Agriculture as well as three members nominated by royal decree from the disciplines of geography, statistics and economics, two other citizens of Rome, and a representative of the Italian Cooperative Societies and of the first aid societies of the major seaport cities.[1] This group was responsible for regulating various matters connected with emigration such as the dissemination of publicity by shipping companies, conditions in ports of departure and prices of voyages.[2]

In connection with its duties, the *Commissariato dell'Emigrazione* published at various times during each year after 1901 a *Bollettino dell'Emigrazione* which provided information both to observers and to potential emigrants.[3] The number of bulletins, their size and contents varied from year to year. Sometimes as many as 22 pamphlets totaling thousands of pages came out in a 12-month period. In other years the publications of the Commissariat were more modest. Their contents covered a wide range of materials from mining conditions in Pennsylvania to land prices in New Zealand, from sleeping arrangements available to emigrants in ports of departure to specifications of what they should be fed during the journey. Among the many reports of Council deliberations and parliamentary debates regarding emigration, an indication appears of how the Italian government responded to repatriation from the United States between 1902 and 1914. Numerous passages refer to the benefits to be derived from temporary emigration.

---

[1] Commissariato dell'Emigrazione, *Bollettino dell'Emigrazione*, no. 10 (1902), 10.

[2] For a discussion of the functions of the Commissariato, see Elizabeth Cometti, "Trends in Italian Emigration," *Western Political Quarterly*, XI (December 1958), 821-22.

[3] The *Bollettino dell'Emigrazione* will hereafter be referred to as the *Bulletin* and the *Commissariato dell'Emigrazione* will be translated as the Commissariat of Emigration.

While the Commissariat perceived advantages for Italy in its impermanent migration, it was aware that Americans did not share in this feeling. Leopoldo Corinaldo, member of the Italian embassy staff in Washington, wrote for publication in the *Bulletin* that Italians were criticized in the United States because they abused the hospitality of their new country when they came in the spring, competed with American workers and left at the beginning of the winter with their small savings. Corinaldo concluded: "It is this class of individuals who are the true 'birds of passage,' who hardly ever spend money here and hate everything which is American except the gold which takes them away."[4]

Aware of the American reaction to temporary emigration, the Commissariat reports before 1904 deemphasized the extent of the return movement from the United States and attempted to show an actual increase in permanent emigrants along with a corresponding decrease in "birds of passage." The *Bulletin* noted:

> The number of repatriates, compared to emigrants, was not high in 1900-1, because a total of 131,656 Italians arrived in New York and of this number only a few more than one-fifth returned. In preceding years the ratio was often one-fourth or one-third of the total. This shows that Italian emigration to the United States is taking on a more permanent character.[5]

The Commissariat pointed out that a slightly higher proportion of women and children were among the emigrants to the United States in the years following 1900. This appeared to indicate that more of those journeying to America intended to remain permanently.[6] After 1904 the Commissariat's statistics on returning Italians showed clearly that temporary emigration was not disappearing, and official publications ceased to make this claim.

The Emigration Act of 1901 offered little protection to repatriating Italians except in cases in which the Italian consular officers concluded that indigent, ill or orphaned emigrants should be aided in their return. Article 25 of the law provided that any Italian in another country who was requested to depart by a diplomatic agent had the privilege of returning to Italy for two *lire* a day including

---

[4] Commissariato dell'Emigrazione, *Bollettino dell'Emigrazione*, no. 1 (1902), 5.

[5] *Ibid.*, no. 1 (1902), 47.

[6] *Ibid.*, no. 2 (1902), 15.

food. Ships had to make this service available based on the number of other passengers they carried and the size of the vessel.[7] The number who returned at the reduced price rarely exceeded five percent of the total of those repatriating, and except for this one provision, reemigration received little attention in the law of 1901.

The bulletins published by the Commissariat of Emigration between 1902 and 1914 indicate official agreement that the same persons participated many times in the migratory movements. As a result, emigration authorities suggested that estimates of returnees based on the total of arrivals in third class accommodations greatly exaggerated the number of individuals involved. Since the Commissariat never attempted to collect statistical information on this matter so as to have some numerical basis for its conclusions, its reports relied on the testimony of observers; their agreement on this point seemed so great as to make other proof unnecessary. Minister of Foreign Affairs, Tommaso Tittoni, after reporting emigration statistics to the lower house of Parliament, concluded: "It is understood that in these figures a person is counted many times."[8] The Commissariat's report for 1906-7 concurred in this judgment:

> It is observed that transoceanic emigration is also assuming an increasingly temporary character . . . . The facilities of communication permit that even emigrants to America can return to Italy to see their families and their native land for two or three years, then leave again to take part in new work. Actual currents of periodic emigration are being formed in some transoceanic countries. Southern peasants, as well as workers from Piedmont, the Veneto and other regions of Italy . . . emigrate about March or April to the United States to do outside construction work, and then they return to Italy at the beginning of the winter season.[9]

Luigi Bodio, Director of the Office of Statistics and a member of the Council on Emigration, urged observers not to worry about reports that large numbers were leaving and returning because many people were counted more than once: "In part, then, the same ones leave again and again."[10]

Whatever the exact number of repatriates, reports of the Commissariat between 1902 and 1914 indicate a general agreement that

---

[7] *Ibid.*, no. 1 (1902), 29.
[8] *Ibid.*, no. 7 (1904), 16.
[9] *Ibid.*, no. 11 (1907), 20.
[10] *Ibid.*, no. 11 (1910), 265.

the *Americani* brought certain advantages to Italy and that official action should both encourage departures and invite returns. In several different passages emigration is referred to as a necessity. In the Foreign Minister's report to the House of Deputies on March 25, 1904, Tittoni stated: "Emigration is a necessity for our country. It would be terrible if this safety valve did not exist, this possibility of finding work elsewhere."[11]

In order to facilitate migration and improve the treatment of those seeking employment in other countries, the Commissariat discussed methods to raise the literacy rate in areas with greatest emigration to the United States. Italian officials knew of the numerous attempts of the United States Congress to pass a literacy test requirement for entering immigrants. The Commissariat pointed out that the approval of such a limitation would have an immediate effect on their population safety valve, and they suggested ways that their government could help adults in parts of southern Italy where illiteracy was particularly high. Bodio, reporting for the Council of Emigration, warned: "On the eve of the new law on immigration in the United States, it should be remembered that 50 percent of our emigrants to North America are illiterate."[12] He asked that his government appropriate a sum of money to be used to establish classes for adults in southern Italy "from where emigration to the United States is greatest."[13] Each failure to pass the literacy requirement was noted with relief by the Commissariat. Bodio wrote: "Since the United States has not yet barred illiterates from immigrating there, the need for Italy to give sums of money to establish classes on Sundays and in the evenings to teach adults to read and write is a less urgent need than before."[14] Bodio warned that the matter needed to be resolved, however, "because the problem [the threat of barring illiterate immigrants from entering the United States] can reappear."[15]

In response to American criticism that Italians were congregating in the large cities of the eastern seaboard, the Commissariat recommended subsidies for the establishment of employment offices in New York in order to inform arriving immigrants of jobs

---

[11] *Ibid.*, no. 7 (1904), 17.
[12] *Ibid.*, no. 9 (1904), 34.
[13] *Ibid.*, no. 11 (1905), 3.
[14] *Ibid.*, no. 9 (1904), 64.
[15] *Ibid.*

available in the interior of the continent and to encourage them to disperse themselves over the entire country. Egisto Rossi, newly appointed head of the Council on Emigration, wrote: "One of our biggest problems now, an urgent problem, is that of achieving a better distribution of Italians in the interior parts of the United States. Only in this way can we both ward off new threats of restrictive legislation and also assure a better situation for our emigrants in the United States."[16]

The encouragement of temporary emigration from Italy to the United States was clearly tied to the matter of money, for the Commissariat reported a direct relationship between temporary emigration and remittances. When Italians settled permanently in another country, their remittances decreased or stopped entirely. Hundreds of pages of the bulletins discuss ways in which to facilitate the transfer of funds between nationals working abroad and their home country. The Emigration Act of January 31, 1901, as amended in February of the same year, assigned to the *Banco di Napoli* the responsibility of forwarding remittances from Italians living in other countries. The law provided: "The service of gathering, using, caring for and transmitting into the kingdom of Italy the savings of its emigrants is given to the *Banco di Napoli*."[17] Each year the Commissariat reported on the functioning of this institution and on the amount of money which it transmitted into Italy. Not all funds went through the Bank, of course, because some workers chose to carry their savings back themselves or to rely on repatriating friends to perform this service.

Although it is, therefore, impossible to be completely accurate about the total amount of money which entered Italy each year from its sons working in other countries, most observers believed the annual figure to be in the millions of dollars. Deputy Gustavo Gavotti, speaking in the lower house of Parliament, estimated that 500 million *lire*, or about 100 million dollars, had entered Italy in the period 1897 to 1902.[18]

The Commissariat of Emigration estimated that between 1902 and 1914 more than 600 million *lire* in remittances entered Italy. Table XXIII shows the amounts sent through various channels each year.

---

[16] *Ibid.*, no. 14 (1905), 22.
[17] *Ibid.*, no. 14 (1905), 107.
[18] *Ibid.*, no. 12 (1904), 33.

TABLE XXIII

REMITTANCES MADE THROUGH THE *BANCO DI NAPOLI* BY ITALIAN EMIGRANTS, 1902-1914: BY METHOD OF TRANSMISSION°

Year	Ordinary remittances to families	Telegraphic remittances	Remittances by Check	Savings Deposited in Bank	Savings Deposited in Post Office	Total
1902	9,304,835.24.	——	——	——	——	9,304,835.24
1903	23,576,694.63	——	——	——	——	23,576,694.63
1904	28,299,399.54	——	——	——	——	28,299,399.54
1905	28,131,981.90	——	——	3,596,911.15	6,688,993.34	38,417,886.39
1906	21,595,891.00	——	——	1,224,124.21	7,068,672.36	29,888,687.57
1907	31,873,961.47	——	——	911,044.77	5,651,299.97	38,441,306.21
1908	24,038,978.63	——	7,100,141.96	856,981.22	4,666,440.90	36,662,542.71
1909	26,496,494.16	——	8,501,846.50	1,004,135.15	4,176,051.49	40,178,527.30
1910	37,775,334.66	——	9,319,615.53	1,880,039.81	8,390,009.43	57,364,999.43
1911	45,346,131.55	——	12,526,164.30	1,150,270.13	9,700,450.74	68,723,016.72
1912	48,039,112.16	1,504,998.75	13,192,376.19	1,628,055.02	11,840,012.56	76,204,554.68
1913	50,146,652.96	2,212,761.00	13,985,248.58	1,921,621.40	16,296,765.74	84,563,049.68
1914	44,284,244.14	10,567,160.97	19,332,994.70	1,262,754.82	9,535,399.60	84,982,554.23

Commissariato Generale dell'Emigrazione, *Annuario Statistico della Emigrazione Italiana dal 1876-1925* (Rome, 1926), 1646.

° In *lire*.

North America was the departure point for more than half of the total sum sent.[19] According to the Commissariat report which was based on information gathered from the *Banco di Napoli*, Italian nationals working in the United States accounted for 43 million *lire* of the total 75 million *lire* transmitted into Italy in 1907-08. The amounts for each year between 1902 and 1914 are shown in Table XXIV.

TABLE XXIV

REMITTANCES FROM ITALIAN EMIGRANTS IN THE UNITED STATES COMPARED TO TOTAL REMITTANCES MADE THROUGH THE *BANCO DI NAPOLI* (in *lire*)

Year	From the United States	Total
1902	7,441,721.89	9,304,835.24
1903	18,567,363.92	23,576,694.63
1904	22,022,384.68	28,299,399.54
1905	27,775,978.53	38,417,886.39
1906	18,440,645.23	29,888,687.57
1907	24,695,591.51	38,441,306.21
1908	18,599,744.90	36,662,542.71
1909	22,253,609.00	40,178,527.30
1910	37,261,778.00	57,364,999.43
1911	48,476,474.12	68,723,016.72
1912	56,558,689.69	76,204,554.68
1913	62,934,813.18	84,563,049.68
1914	66,040,736.77	84,982,554.23

Commissariato Generale dell'Emigrazione, *Annuario Statistico della Emigrazione Italiana dal 1876-1925* (Rome, 1925), 1647-1648.

It was the unusual emigrant who returned to Italy without a small nestegg. Luigi Rossi, a member of the Council on Emigration, reported to the Minister of Foreign Affairs:

One can say, almost with certainty, that compared to the great number of those who gain evident benefits from their expatriation, the number is negligible of workers who spend a certain number of years abroad without having any positive result. Repatriates from abroad frequently return with between 1,000 and 5,-000 *lire*. Sometimes the amount is as high as 10,000 *lire*. The savings are generally proportional to the length of the stay abroad.[20]

[19] *Ibid.*, no. 18 (1910), 388-89.
[20] *Ibid.*, no. 18 (1910), 45.

The Commissariat, having noted the large amount of money funneled into Italy from nationals working abroad, pointed out that the funds were not distributed evenly over the country. Southern Italy got nearly two-thirds of the total remittances, the *Bulletin* reported, because of the fact that so many from the *Mezzogiorno* had chosen to go to the United States.[21]

After providing for the transmission of funds into Italy, the group in charge of regulating emigration considered the use of these moneys and their effect on the country. The first conclusion to emerge from the investigations pointed to the consequence on real estate values, because land prices rose as remittances increased. Luigi Rossi, in his report to the Minister of Foreign Affairs, summarized the results of a survey of mayors in southern Italian towns:

> According to the news, which is nearly unanimous, furnished to the Commissariat by the mayors of different towns, the increased demand for land on the part of the emigrants . . . has noticeably influenced land prices. In some areas such as Veneto, Campania, Apulia, Calabria and Sicily, there has arisen the business of buying and selling land. Able speculators, foreseeing the return of the emigrants, acquire large amounts of land at a low price, and after cutting it up into convenient units, they resell the land at a very high price to the repatriates.[22]

Since many of the returned were able to acquire land of their own, they were less willing to work for others, and the result was that labor costs increased. Of the southern towns with largest emigration and return, Rossi noted:

> The increase in wages makes the condition of the small landowners who are not cultivators more difficult. Almost all the mayors in southern Italy echoed the general distaste of this class of citizens for emigration which has taken from them the possibility of cultivating land in a way so as to obtain profitable results.[23]

Rossi's own opinion was that the long-range result of this development would serve to change the economic and social structure of those parts of the country involved. He wrote:

---

[21] *Ibid.*, no. 18 (1910), 381.
[22] *Ibid.*, no. 18 (1910), 47.
[23] *Ibid.*

The situation [in which landowners find themselves without cheap labor] constrains them either to change the cultivation so that it is less intensive or else to sell their property, and this, which at first sight seemed an ill, constitutes a fountain of beneficial change for the national economy since the landowners of southern Italy are required now to look for better ways of competing for workers.[24]

Other typical investments of the returning emigrants included constructing new homes or starting small businesses. Rossi reported:

Some mayors of towns in the parts in which migratory movements are strongest give thanks to emigration which has permitted the raising up of clean and happy houses of the repatriates. Often the result is a completely new section of a town, making a strange contrast to the unhealthy caves of the less well-to-do.[25]

Other returning Italians, Rossi reported, chose to invest their savings in animals or small agricultural businesses, and in northern Italy, skilled workmen sometimes joined other repatriates from the same area and opened up small shops.[26]

Rossi concluded that all sections he examined except one benefited from the remittances and investments of the returned. Basilicata, an inland region in the south of the peninsula, had been for years one of the most depressed areas in all of Italy, and it received little help from its returned ones. Rossi lamented:

Nor do the remittances of the emigrants tend to change these conditions in Basilicata. The savings, in fact, are not ever invested in land and, therefore, do not help, as they do in other areas, to break up landed estates and raise the condition of agriculture. The workers emigrating from Basilicata repatriate only for a short time and prefer to deposit their nesteggs in a savings bank so they can emigrate again more easily.[27]

The Commissariat attached primary importance to the economic effects of temporary emigration, results which did not come from permanent population loss. Giovanni Casattini, observer and student of emigration, wrote for the *Bulletin:*

---

[24] *Ibid.*
[25] *Ibid.*, no. 18 (1910), 48.
[26] *Ibid.*
[27] *Ibid.*, no. 18 (1910), 49.

> Permanent emigration represents . . . a bloody wound, behind
> which are prolonged and reproduced the causes of its origin be-
> cause it renders nothing to the population that feeds it. The
> temporary emigrants, instead, . . . compete among themselves
> to search for remedies and to ameliorate the grievous economic
> conditions, permanent or transitory, that drove them out of their
> country.[28]

One sector of the economy benefiting most directly from migration was Italian shipping. Before 1900 Italian carriers did not
serve large numbers of emigrants, but the Commissariat reported
with satisfaction after the turn of the century that increasing numbers of their compatriots chose ships of their country's flag. Italian
carriers found it a convenient arrangement to transport large numbers of emigrants in both directions on the Atlantic. The Commissariat reported:

> It is noted that while the number of emigrants leaving Italy is
> climbing, the total of repatriates remains high . . . . Those
> returning constituted a third of those that left. As a result, ships of
> the Italian line were assured a considerable number of passengers
> also for the return voyages.[29]

To protect the increasing number of repatriates, as well as
assure that their country's ships got a greater share of returning
traffic, the Italian government imposed license requirements and
other regulations on all foreign vessels carrying passengers in third
class accommodations to its ports. In debating the proposal, the
Council noted:

> Some regulation of return voyages is indicated because, besides
> being in the interest of the emigrants, it would also help Italian
> carriers which are exposed on the return trip to sharp competition
> from foreign companies that are not under controls, and, avoiding
> every kind of responsibility, are able to take from our carriers a
> great deal of business. This is a fact worthy of attention since the
> repatriation of emigrants constitutes one of the principal elements
> of traffic at this time.[30]

The change proposed by the Council provided:

---

[28] *Ibid.*, no. 3 (1904), 94.
[29] *Ibid.*, no. 10 (1905), 13.
[30] *Ibid.*, no. 8 (1907), 17.

The transportation of emigrants who repatriate can be exercised only by ships holding a permit or by companies that have obtained a special license. Such license will be issued on the following conditions: (1) that the transportation occurs in the same conditions as those specified in the Emigration Act of 1901 (for the journey to America) and (2) that a tax be paid for every passenger disembarking in the kingdom.[31]

Some members of the Council objected that the group assumed extraterritorial powers if it imposed conditions on ships sailing from other countries. One member of the Council, Francesco Saverio Nitti, added that returning emigrants were considerably wiser than when they had left Italy and that they had little need for this kind of protection.[32] Nitti noted, in addition, that the cost of the tax would be passed on to the ticket buyer by the shipping company and the repatriates would suffer.[33]

In discussing the proposed requirement that conditions on returning voyages be equivalent to those on westward bound ships, the Council recommended:

On the returning voyages there are a great number of repatriating nationals. It would be a good idea for physicians and inspectors to adopt the same diligence on the return trip as on the voyages to America, being careful so that the treatment of passengers, whether in food or hygiene is that prescribed in the emigration legislation of 1901.[34]

By extending to return voyages the protection granted in the earlier law, the Council members assured their repatriating countrymen of a safer journey. The 1901 legislation had set specific standards for hygienic conditions and medical care in third class travel. The law required that doctors be available on each ship and specified the exact amount of medical supplies which were to be aboard, including the number of footbaths and ounces of gauze per 1000 passengers.[35] Detailed menus instructed the ships' cooks of the minimum requirements for steerage travelers and further specified:

---

[31] *Ibid.*, no. 12 (1907), 55.
[32] *Ibid.*, no. 12 (1907), 56.
[33] *Ibid.*
[34] *Ibid.*, no. 5 (1903), 69.
[35] *Ibid.*, no. 14 (1904), 46f.

"Cheese used as a condiment must be Italian and of good quality. That which is served with bread can be Dutch."[36]

When the Council on Emigration approved both sections of the law, it provided a more pleasant return trip for the repatriates and increased its own revenue. It had not yet dealt, however, with the one serious, remaining complaint of repatriates who protested that they could never be sure of the date of departure on returning voyages. They reported that they sometimes bought tickets for a ship scheduled to sail on a certain date and went to the port in preparation for leaving. Instead, they were informed that the ship would leave at the carrier's convenience meaning that the passengers were forced to stay nearby at their own expense until sailing time. In proposing changes in the 1901 Act, the Council requested that sanctions be applied to ships which did not adhere to the sailing date printed on the tickets.[37] In addition, the group recommended that ships carrying repatriates be required to take the passengers directly to an Italian port if they had not been informed before purchasing their tickets that there would be intermediary stops.[38]

The Commissariat had assumed, under the 1901 Act, the regulation of price limits on tickets to the New World. In effect, the maximum allowed became the minimum or accepted charge. The Council's authority did not extend to the regulation of return fares, but that problem was less acute since competition among shipping companies seeking to carry the returning passengers, who usually numbered fewer than those traveling westward, tended to moderate the charges. In one case, a price war lowered the cost of a return journey from the United States to 40 *lire*, or less than eight dollars and about one-third the usual price.[39]

The Commissariat's bulletins pointed to various changes in the *Americani*. Evidence was cited, for example, that residence in the United States altered habits of hygiene. Medical Colonel A. Montano, officer in charge of those attending the ills of returning emigrants, noted: "Doctors report that on the going trip few emigrants took baths but on the return voyage almost all the children and a good part of the adults bathed because of the importance

---

[36] *Ibid.*, no. 14 (1904), 62.
[37] *Ibid.*, no. 5 (1903), 13.
[38] *Ibid.*, no. 5 (1903), 14.
[39] *Ibid.*, no. 9 (1908), 165.

given, especially in North America and even among the working classes, to keeping themselves very clean."[40]

Luigi Rossi reported to other member of the Council:

> In general the repatriates from the United States return to Italy with a patrimony of hygienic knowledge and show greater care for themselves. Especially those who have had the opportunity to work in the great factories on the other side of the ocean where hygiene is valued greatly become efficient propaganda sources to make known to our working class that familiarity with water improves a person's health.[41]

Those returning from the United States, besides giving more importance to cleanliness, were believed to value education more highly than did their compatriots who had never left. The bulletins published more than one bit of evidence for this conclusion. Luigi Rossi reported that many had noted that the repatriate "who has had the experience of observing the greater respect that comes to literate workers is often the best support of the teacher and pushes and persuades his own children to learn in order to furnish them with a weapon from which they can profit all their lives."[42] When 147 mayors of southern towns were asked whether the returnees showed interest in their children's education, 125 reported that they did and 22 said they did not.[43] Often the returned adults enrolled in classes in order to further their education.[44]

The Commissariat reported that some emigrants, while away from their country, had been impressed with the importance of participating in civic activities in order to promote their own interests. Rossi wrote:

> The observing of the workers in other countries who actively participate in public life as the best way of defending their own interests pushes our workers to attribute more importance to elections, and this consciousness in our citizens is proved especially by the considerable number of emigrants . . . who return in the election periods . . . with the objective of participating in the selection of members of Parliament.[45]

---

[40] *Ibid.*, no. 21 (1908), 87.
[41] *Ibid.*, no. 18 (1910), 49.
[42] *Ibid.*, no. 18 (1910), 50.
[43] *Ibid.*, no. 12 (1909), 126.
[44] *Ibid.*, no. 18 (1910), 50.
[45] *Ibid.*, no. 18 (1910), 51.

The effect of temporary emigration on crime rates in Italy was less clear. Luigi Rossi concluded, in the absence of statistics on the matter, that the better economic conditions of the repatriates modified their tendency to be delinquent.[46] By removing many of the unemployed, emigration helped to decrease crimes of certain kinds, especially those against property, but it may have increased crimes against persons since the emigrants were reported to return with the habit of carrying weapons.[47]

In addition to a possible influence on crime rates, the repatriates brought other problems to blight the remittances that Italy eagerly sought. While the Commissariat reports noted that nationals returning from the United States funneled their savings into the home country, boosted Italian shipping, helped change the land system, publicized better health habits and gave more importance to education, the bulletins also reported numerous problems resulting from temporary residence abroad.

The most common complaint against the repatriates was that they brought with them illnesses. Doctors attending emigrants on the trans-Atlantic crossings observed that the rate of sickness was clearly higher among the homeward bound than for those traveling westward. Several possible explanations existed to account for this difference, and the bulletins noted some of them. Sick people, nostalgic for their families or their birthplace, undertook the return trip when their health was precarious. Seriously ill individuals may have concealed their condition on the westward trip because of the careful and well-publicized inspection of immigrants arriving in the United States. For many of those involved the return voyage signified failure or unrealized ambitions. As a result of these and other causes, the number of both physical and mental illnesses treated on return voyages far exceeded those of travelers going to the western hemisphere. Table XXV shows the number of reported illnesses and deaths among third class passengers traveling between North America and Italy in the years 1903 through 1906.

Tuberculosis was the most common illness among those returning from North America. Table XXVI shows the number of cases of the most common diseases treated on ocean voyages in 1904 when there were more persons suffering from tuberculosis on the return trips than from all other illnesses combined. In 1905 doc-

---

[46] *Ibid.*, no. 18 (1910), 52.
[47] *Ibid.*

TABLE XXV

REPORTED RATE OF ILLNESS AND DEATH AMONG
ITALIANS TRAVELING THIRD CLASS BETWEEN ITALY
AND THE UNITED STATES, 1903-1906
(PER 1000 PASSENGERS)

Year	*ILLNESSES* Going to U.S.	Returning from U.S.
1903	9.86	14.13
1904	6.98	10.89
1905	8.17	17.80
1906	7.15	17.02

Year	*DEATHS* Going to U.S.	Returning from U.S.
1903	.19	.63
1904	.15	.41
1905	.14	.49
1906	.16	.58

Commissariato dell'Emigrazione, *Bollettino dell'Emigrazione*, no. 2 (1908), 148.

tors reported only one case of tuberculosis among emigrants going
to the United States, but 350 among those returning.[48]
    The number of mentally ill treated on return voyages also
exceeded that of those going to North America. When this figure is
expressed as a percentage of the thousands of persons involved, the
rate difference is considerable, since many more went to America
than returned. Colonel Montano reported to the Commissariat that
in 1906 only one case of mental illness was reported among the
thousands traveling third class to America. On the return, however,
72 sought treatment for mental disorders, including 55 men and 15
women.[49]
    One part of this phenomenon was manifested in the greater
number of suicides on the return voyages. Dr. T. Rosati, reporting
his observations of hygienic and sanitary conditions of transoceanic
travel, concluded: "There were two suicides on the return trip and

[48] *Ibid.*, no. 4 (1907), 67.
[49] *Ibid.*, no. 2 (1908), 146.

TABLE XXVI

NUMBER OF CASES TREATED AMONG
ITALIANS IN THIRD CLASS TRAVEL BETWEEN
THE UNITED STATES AND ITALY IN 1904

Illness	Going to U.S.	Returning to Italy
Measles	72	47
Scarlet fever	2	2
Chicken pox	12	11
Smallpox	9	2
Diphtheria	0	12
Mumps	10	11
Whooping cough	4	0
Pneumonia	45	16
Tuberculosis	0	278
Meningitis	5	1
Typhoid	11	11
Malaria	61	49
Syphilis	4	8
Ringworm	0	3
Scabies	20	20
Conjunctivitis	0	10
Other	8	22
Total	263	503

Commissariato dell'Emigrazione, *Bollettino dell'Emigrazione*, no. 20 (1905), 28.

this is something to think about—that suicide is more frequent among the repatriates. The causes are many. Certainly these deaths from suicide on the return voyages are in direct relation to the number of mentally ill who come back from North America."[50]

Those who returned from the United States were judged, however, to have a slight advantage over some of the other repatriates. Luigi Rossi wrote that he had heard the returnees described at the port of Genoa in this way:

Whoever has experience . . . can distinguish at first sight who comes from Brazil, who from Argentina and who from the United States by the individual's physiognomy, his actions and his dress . . . . A mayor of one town told me that those returning from the United States come with sufficient health and money, those from Argentina return with their health but little money, and those from Brazil bring neither health nor money.[51]

---

[50] *Ibid.*, no. 16 (1910), 13.
[51] *Ibid.*, no. 9 (1913), 60.

Some observers complained that the *Americani* came back with habits of excessive drinking and gambling. When Luigi Villari, consular agent attached to emigration services, reported on Italians living in Philadelphia, he abhorred the drinking customs of his compatriots: "What is worse is that the moral effects of emigration are not limited to those who stay in America but are eventually introduced into Italy by the repatriates . . . so that alcoholism, a previously unknown habit among our rural population, is already beginning to spread in all the provinces of great emigration."[52] Villari concluded that it was advisable to discourage emigration to Philadelphia since "if we reflect on the moral consequences of the state of things, we cannot avoid the conclusion that even the savings and remittances, which the emigrants send back, can be paid for too dearly."[53]

In the survey of 147 mayors of southern towns, opinion was divided: 70 said that the returnees brought back bad drinking and gambling habits while 77 said that they did not.[54] Rosati, in his report to the Commissariat, took the position that although repatriates returned with a greater taste for liquor, they brought other, more important, qualities: "We do not exclude that drinkers of whisky and brandy return to Italy. We think, however, that among the repatriates there are also those acquainted with soap, with meat, and with the alphabet, and we are satisfied with the counterbalance."[55]

In addition to these specific problems, members of Parliament reported a general dissatisfaction among the repatriates in their home districts. Pasquale Villari, speaking before his colleagues in the Senate, said:

> Many people see Italian emigration to the United States in different ways. The landowner in southern Italy says it has increased wages and caused difficulty in finding labor. Others are pleased with the dollars that are sent back. But while everybody is talking of these dollars, it must be remembered that Italians going to the United States take with them 40 or 50 dollars each and, more than that, they take their health, youth, and vigor . . . . Then these men return from abroad, unable to work in the fields. They dis-

---

[52] *Ibid.*, no. 16 (1908), 48.
[53] *Ibid.*
[54] *Ibid.*, no. 12 (1909), 126.
[55] *Ibid.*, no. 16 (1909), 31.

parage their country. They cannot get used to the modest life of our people . . . . They return with a few dollars, with five or six thousand *lire,* and buy a house, but they are unable to adapt to the life of our people. They return three or four times to America where they end up Americanized or else stay in Italy where they are of little use as citizens.[56]

Villari's was not the prevailing opinion among members of the upper house of Parliament. Senator Giustino Fortunato was one of several to speak more favorably of the working habits of the repatriates. He said that the truth was that the craftsmen refused to accept jobs beneath the level for which they had been trained but that agricultural workers returned willingly to till the soil.[57]

Opinion was unanimous on the effect of temporary emigration on family life. The absence of the father from the home was repeatedly blamed in the publications of the Commissariat for a whole list of evils. Luigi Rossi's report was just one example:

The judgment is unanimous among those asked, even among those considering emigration from an optimistic point of view, that it constitutes a grave menace for the firmness of family ties . . . . Emigration has, in part, contributed to the increased number of cases of adultery, of illegitimate births, of abortions, of infanticides and of the series of crimes that are linked to the weakening of the family structure.[58]

Often children left school to seek employment at a young age in order to substitute for the missing wages of the absent father.[59] The total effect on family life was judged by Italian officials to be harmful for their country.

In spite of its disadvantages, repatriation from the United States received general approval in the publications of the Commissariat of Emigration between 1902 and 1914. The benefits thought to be derived from the return migration, especially the remittances, far outweighed the problems it brought. Deputy Paolo Falletti, speaking in the lower house of Parliament, voiced the opinion which predominated in many discourses of his colleagues when he said: "Repatriation is certainly an advantage for us, be-

---

[56] *Ibid.,* no. 12 (1909), 95f.
[57] *Ibid.,* no. 12 (1909), 107.
[58] *Ibid.,* no. 18 (1910), 53.
[59] *Ibid.,* no. 18 (1910), 54.

cause it represents what permanent emigration does not . . . . Because of this, I maintain that we must preserve ever stronger the ties of the mother country with our emigrants in order to facilitate their return."[60]

Falletti specifically recommended that his government appropriate 200,000 *lire* for schools in the United States to teach nationals better Italian and strengthen their attachment to the mother country.[61] Although other members of Parliament made similar suggestions, institutions for the specific purpose of preserving emigrants' ties with Italy were never established in North America.[62]

Much of the work that would have been done by such schools was already being accomplished by emigrant aid societies which operated in major cities in the United States. These philanthropic agencies varied in personnel and objectives. Some established hospitals and ministered to the sick; others gathered information on jobs and gave advice on family problems to Italians living abroad.[63] The directors of one of the societies, the *Istituto di San Raffaele*, summarized their objectives: "The purpose of the Society of San Raffaele is to keep alive in the hearts of Italians the Catholic faith and with it the sentiment of nationality and affection for the mother country."[64]

The Council on Emigration regularly appropriated to several of these societies a share of the Fund for Emigration which was derived, in part, from a tax on the ship tickets of emigrants. In 1905, for example, three New York organizations received a total appropriation of 68,000 *lire* from the Fund: 35,000 *lire* went to the *Società per gli Immigranti Italiani*, 25,000 *lire* to the *Istituto di Beneficenza* and 8,000 *lire* to the *Società di San Raffaele*.[65]

The Council on Emigration also encouraged repatriation in other, more direct, ways. After July, 1906, reduced train fares were available to both emigrants and repatriates between their homes in Italy and port cities.[66]

---

[60] *Ibid.*, no. 15 (1905), 147.
[61] *Ibid.*
[62] *Ibid.*, no. 1 (1907), 21.
[63] *Ibid.*, no. 14 (1905), 74.
[64] Antonio Perotti, "La Società Italiana e le Prime Migrazioni di Massa," in Centro di Studi Emigrazione, *Studi Emigrazion* (Rome, 1968), 101.
[65] Commissariato dell'Emigrazione, *Bollettino dell'Emigrazione*, no. 14 (1905), 74.
[66] *Ibid.*, no. 11 (1907), 145.

Italians abroad who were considering returning were repeatedly assured of their welcome. Foreign Minister Tittoni reminded them on one occasion: "We sincerely advise Italians who go to search for work in the United States that, if they return, the mother country will never refuse to recognize them as her sons."[67] This view was codified in the law of June 13, 1912, which provided for the easy resumption of Italian citizenship by nationals who had become citizens of another country. Renewing Italian citizenship cost nothing, and it could be accomplished by returning to reside in Italy for two years.[68]

The Italian government continued to seek new ways to encourage repatriation. In a long speech before Parliament on the effects on Italy of emigration, Senator Edoardo Pantano summed up the response of his government to repatriation from the United States and the view represented in the *Bulletin of Emigration* between 1902 and 1914: "The great current of returning emigrants represents an economic force of the first order for us. It will be an enormous benefit for us if we can increase this flow of force in and out of our country . . . if we can increase this temporary emigration."[69]

---

[67] *Ibid.*, no. 7 (1904), 115.
[68] Foerster, *The Italian Emigration*, 490.
[69] Commissariato dell'Emigrazione, *Bollettino dell'Emigrazione*, no. 11 (1910), 226.

4

Repatriates' Impressions of the United States: 1900-1914

THE ITALIANS who repatriated from the United States between 1900 and 1914 carried with them impressions and opinions not necessarily coincident with those expressed by their government in the publications of the Commissariat of Emigration. The individuals involved in the exchange of men for dollars viewed their contribution to the process somewhat differently than the persons who facilitated the transfers between the two countries.

Most emigrants did not record their experiences in America. More than half of them were illiterate, and those who could write letters home with their precious remittances did not deal at length with judgments of life in the United States or with comparisons between their new city and the *paese* they had left. Their brief epistles concentrated on their own health, their hopes for the well-being of the recipients and the amount of money they were earning.[1]

In the absence of published accounts by masses of unskilled laborers, reports of atypical temporary emigrants who did record their experiences were examined to arrive at a conclusion on the main differences observed between the two countries. These better-educated returnees included physicians, priests, professors and government officials. They did not necessarily speak for the unskilled emigrant who journeyed to North America in search of bread. Few of the professionals experienced quite the same confusion that the workers described undergoing during their transoceanic crossing, their arrival in a strange city and their difficulties finding and keeping a job. The comments of the more educated emigrants and observers illustrate, however, some common Italian reactions to the United States and generally resemble the recollections of unschooled repatriates who consented to interviews.

Gaetano Conte, one of the university-educated emigrants who returned after a sojourn in the United States, wrote of leaving Genoa in 1893 with his family in order to raise his five children in "a free country."[2] Conte worked in Boston for a protective society for Italian workers until he was accused of profiting personally from funds set aside to help immigrants. After ten years of ministering to

---

[1] Italians who emigrated to Northern Europe after World War II show a similar unwillingness to make judgments. For an examination of some of their letters, see Arrigo Bongiorno and Aldo Barbina, *Il Pane degli Altri* (Milan, 1971).

[2] Gaetano Conte, *Dieci Anni in America* (Palermo, 1903), 2.

laborers more typical of the mass migration than himself, he ventured some conclusions on the adjustment of Italian immigrants in America.

Conte noted that many of the workers expressed a close attachment to both the country they had left and the one in which they had found work. He cited as an example of this divided patriotism one Italian worker whom he met on a train between Boston and New York. In Conte's words the worker expressed his love for America this way:

> I love America for the democratic spirit of its institutions, for its daring talent, for the feverish activity which dominates here. I love it for its practical, helpful religious faith. I admire it for its size, its resources, the nobility of its ambitions. And I love it for the good that it has done for me and that it does for the hundreds of our workers and those from other countries who find here in America exile, work and civility.[3]

The worker finished by asking Conte what it was that caused him to return permanently to Italy. Conte answered: "Oh I love Italy for its customs and speech, for the sweat that costs me, the air, the land, the rocks."[4]

Not wanting to disagree entirely with Conte but desiring to make his own point clear, the worker interrupted: "I love Italy too, but I love her as my mother, the cause of my existence, and this does not prevent me from loving America as my wife, the cause of my present happiness."[5]

Conte believed that Italians remained more closely attached to their home country than any other immigrant group in the United States. He wrote: "The language, the religion, the traditions and the hope of return are all strong ties for the emigrant. A favorite phrase among the Italian immigrants is 'Italy is always Italy.' "[6]

Diomede Carito, a physician who resided briefly in the United States in 1910, noted the same division of loyalty among Italians living in America. He reported seeing his countrymen existing on the minimal necessities so they could send more money to the families they had left in Italy. One of these men said to Carito:

---

[3] *Ibid.*, 204.
[4] *Ibid.*, 205.
[5] *Ibid.*
[6] *Ibid.*, 85.

"Doctor, we brought to America only our brains and our arms. Our hearts stayed there in the little houses in the beautiful fields of our Italy."[7]

Most observers lamented this situation in which men lived alternately in two countries, not entirely content in either. Italy could not give them jobs, and life in America did not suit them. Luigi Villari, Italian Consul in Philadelphia, expressed satisfaction with this division of loyalty among his countrymen because it led, in his opinion, to slow assimilation and eventual repatriation. He wrote:

> The Italian immigrant in the United States is not disposed to Americanize himself and, from our point of view, this is his best quality. The Italians of the first generation conserve their national characteristics since they live in an ambient absolutely separate from the Americans. The workers and miners, even though ignorant, are doubtlessly among the best of our emigrants and we should be glad that they are so difficult to assimilate and that so many of them repatriate.[8]

Besides agreeing on the division of loyalty among Italian workers, most of the published reports of temporary residence in the United States between 1900 and 1914 concurred in the superiority of several aspects of life in North America. Several of them praised the new country so generously that their writings appear to be publicity tracts encouraging immigration.

Gherardo Ferreri, an ear, nose and throat specialist, wrote enthusiastically of the America he observed in 1906:

> Whoever desires to travel will never feel the great desire to return to the place he has seen [so much] as the person who goes to the United States. I would like to be able to persuade, either with pen or with spoken word, those who are able to move to pass over Europe and go to the United States to learn what is lacking in Italy.[9]

Ferreri commended particularly the education system which, in his opinion, allowed young people to mature earlier:

---

[7] Diomede Carito, *Nella Terra di Washington: Le Mie Visioni della Psiche Nord America* (Naples, 1912), 104.

[8] Luigi Villari, *Gli Stati Uniti d'America e l'Emigrazione Italiana* (Milan, 1912), 290.

[9] Gherardo Ferreri, *Gli Italiani in America* (Rome, 1907), 13-14.

The characteristic passion of the North American people for arduous undertakings which others would not dare to attempt in politics, religion and sports is, in my opinion, the mature fruit of a perfect education in youth in which everything is intended to develop the joys of work and of life, the sense of beauty and of dignity and the moral concepts which made of man a superior being in a living world.[10]

Piero Barbera, a Florentine newsman who worked in the United States briefly in 1903, also praised American schools which turned out, in his opinion, superior workers. Barbera noted that the effects reached into the printing industry and helped account for the high level of work which he observed being accomplished:

Every worker on a book, first of all, knows what a book is because he not only produces it but also consumes it. This is a truth which explains many things . . . . The workers search for scientific knowledge in order to perfect their work. The most modest laborer has a general culture superior to the average of ours. They know how to write, they know geography and history. They know how to draw, and they do not have that crass ignorance concerning natural phenomena which even persons of high literary culture possess among us.[11]

Several Italian observers noted that even humble Americans worked out objectives for their lives and considered their own determination and hard work the most important factors in reaching these goals. Diomede Carito wrote:

The North American, from the farmer to the university graduate, has a program for his life from which he does not deviate . . . . Life in America takes place, for the most part, under the rule of will and only in a minimal way under the rule of sentiment . . . . School teachers instruct every North American boy that the most beautiful word in the dictionary is duty and the highest manifestation of duty is work.[12]

Ferreri lauded the American political system and predicted that exposure to it would influence Italian workers who returned to their homeland:

[10] *Ibid.*, 12.
[11] Piero Barbera, *Editori e Autori: Studi e Passatempi di un Libraio* (Florence, 1904), 271.
[12] Carito, *Nella Terra di Washington*, 134-38.

Democracy [in America] lays a foundation in the Italian-Americans who return to Italy. They will learn how to stir up national public opinion and push the country toward a government capable of resolving the great economic and social problems which have spread in the peninsula including the plague of malaria, unemployment and the flight across the Atlantic of millions of workers.[13]

Ferreri judged southern Italian workers living in America to be inferior to native-born New Englanders in hygiene, morals and education. After a visit to a Massachusetts farm, Ferreri concluded: "The most humble Anglo-Saxon farmer deserves honor and admiration as a model of order, cleanliness and elegance."[14]

Alberto Pecorini, an Italian professor who resided temporarily in Massachusetts, noted a few imperfections in the America of 1908. He praised the rapid industrialization of the United States but observed that both economic and social problems resulted. He deplored the development of trusts and monopolies as well as the acceptance of the inevitability of industrial accidents, the employment of children in factories and the overcrowding in cities "with the consequent physical deterioration of a great part of the population."[15] Pecorini marveled:

It is strange that the country which values most highly the individual and his rights is also the one which neglects human life, calculating it too often in dollars. Many companies prefer to put into a small account a certain sum to pay widows and orphans of the unfortunate [workers injured on their jobs] rather than diminish their production or introduce costly systems to reduce or prevent accidents.[16]

Pecorini deplored the treatment of his countrymen and their children in the factories:

In New Jersey children of Italian immigrants fill the glass factories. They are little martyrs who begin to work at ten or 12 years of age and die ten or 12 years later with tuberculosis . . . . The result is that 150,000 die each year from tuberculosis and other diseases. And, as though this were not enough, the flocking to the

---

[13] Ferreri, *Gli Italiani in America*, 16.
[14] *Ibid.*, 87.
[15] Alberto Pecorini, *Gli Americani nella Vita Moderna* (Milan, 1909), 161.
[16] *Ibid.*

cities continues so that they are not now anything more than enormous conglomerations of factories and streets full of dust and noise in which from every side a population full of neurasthenics flees or runs or hurls itself searching frantically for money. The Americans eat too quickly and do not digest. They sleep too little and do not rest. They keep every nerve tense enough to break, and their minds are continually agitated, like the lava of a volcano, with the hope and the business of tomorrow. Every year Americans take great amounts of patent medicine, the contents of which they do not even know, in order to calm their nerves so they can continue the race and win at the end their objective of prosperity. Then they die.[17]

In spite of the disastrous effects of rapid industrialization, Pecorini believed that America's future was bright. He concluded optimistically:

The United States has not yet known its success, its victory, its wealth. It must mature to know delusions and more bitter encounters. These are the experiences which create in a people that profound sense of reality without which a nation cannot understand itself. Young people of Europe, America has more energy than its mother and fewer prejudices . . . . America will reach its destiny.[18]

Italy's Senator Antonio di San Giuliano praised the democratic spirit which he observed during an extended visit to the United States:

One of the impressions that I brought from the United States is that the psychological part of de Tocqueville's book is still true today as it was 74 years ago and that the average American of 1905 is, in his essential characteristics, about the same as de Tocqueville saw in 1831.[19]

Diomede Carito and other writers agreed that the relationships they observed between persons of different social classes in America contrasted greatly with what they had been accustomed to seeing in Italy. Carito noted: "What impressed me most of all during my first stay [in the United States] was the reciprocal

---

[17] *Ibid.*
[18] *Ibid.*, 414-15.
[19] Antonio di San Giuliano, "L'Emigrazione Italiana negli Stati Uniti," *Nuova Antologia*, CXVIII (July-August 1905), 96.

dignity in the relationships between persons of high and low social classes."[20]

Professors, physicians and senators who published their own observations on life in the United States between 1900 and 1914 did not represent the unskilled, illiterate workers who comprised the largest part of the mass migration. Their writings indicate, however, a general agreement on the most striking differences encountered by individuals who lived in both countries. Each of the two lands seemed to offer advantages and liabilities to the people involved.

The writings examined generally praised American life, especially its schools, its political system and its factories which furnished jobs to unskilled workers, but they deplored some of the features accompanying industrialization. Several educated Italian immigrants observed favorably a social system which made fewer class distinctions than they had been accustomed to seeing in their own country. Most writers expressed confusion and discomfort with the noise and bustle of large American cities. All of those cited, in spite of their praise for life in the United States, returned to Italy.

Although unrepresentative of the typical emigrant to the United States before 1914, the writers whose works were examined did not differ greatly in their impressions from the uneducated returnees who were interviewed. Most of those repatriating before 1914 are no longer alive to recount their experiences, and those who survive often do not remember clearly their life in the United States more than half a century ago. A small group of respondents and possible inaccuracies in their answers constituted only two of the problems involved in attempting to interview repatriates and their families concerning the effects of residence in America.

Suspicion of questions from strangers formed a considerable barrier, especially in southern Italy where most of the repatriates reside. Almost all the returnees and their families who discussed their experiences and impressions requested that their names be changed or omitted. Anonymity appeared to provide them with a protective shield behind which subsequent changes of mind, inaccurate reminiscences or, possibly, reasons for flight could be obscured. This insistence on secrecy often prevented the recounting of what seemed to be the most harmless detail, especially if the

---

[20] Carito, *Nella Terra di Washington*, 140.

question was a specific one. A general inquiry regarding returnees, if asked over a pizza and between comments on the weather or the culinary specialities, was acceptable. A more specific question on the exact place of residence or the occupation exercised in the United States was often rejected entirely.

In some cases, persons questioned in southern Italy refused to acknowledge that they knew even one returnee. A uniformed policeman, for example, in a small town in Reggio Calabria, which reportedly regained 50 percent of its emigrants to the United States between 1900 and 1914, maintained that he could not recall hearing of any individual who had come back before World War I. He insisted that any information on returnees would have to come from the Mayor or his assistant, both of whom were unavailable.

Other southern Italians discussed somewhat more willingly the effect of America on countrymen who had returned. Gaetano Colella, a librarian in Agrigento's municipal library, could find in the city's collection no written record of emigration to the United States except two volumes of poetry written in "*Americano*" as Colella referred to the language spoken in North America. When questioned regarding personal acquaintances who might have talked of their experiences, Colella finally volunteered the information that his father had migrated to Brooklyn, New York in 1905.[21] He returned to Agrigento five years later and never expressed any desire to go back to America except to visit relatives in 1931.

"My father went as a young man," Gaetano Colella explained, "eager to find a better life than he had had here. Instead he found a city full of noise and chaos so he came back to Agrigento. He never encouraged any of his sons to emigrate because he knew that the better life was here in Sicily."[22]

When asked what difference his father's emigration and repatriation had made to his life and that of his family, Colella pointed out that his father had encouraged his children to continue their education beyond the university. The elder Colella had enrolled in classes when he returned to Agrigento in order to become a mechanic instead of a common laborer. The librarian recalled that his father often traveled several miles in order to attend a theatrical performance. He was proud of the English he had learned in

---

[21] Gaetano Colella [pseud.] to author, June 23, 1971.
[22] *Ibid.*

Brooklyn, and during World War II when the Americans were in Sicily he demonstrated that he could still speak his second language more than 30 years after he had left New York.

Antonio Colella's death in 1961 caused his son to consider carefully the effect of his father's temporary residence in Brooklyn. "My father went to New York intending to remain," he said, "but he returned disillusioned with the noise and confusion. As the years passed he forgot his disappointment and remembered only the extravagances of the experience. Perhaps it was there that he could buy his first suit of clothes. He always spoke of America as a very big and different place, much as one might speak of a noisy festival that one has attended in order to brag of being present rather than for any enjoyment in the event itself."[23]

The younger Colella expressed no desire to see the United States except for "perhaps a few Indian caves." He repeatedly referred to the superiority of life in Sicily where he believed people lived happier, more tranquil lives.

Antonio Colella's objections to the noise and confusion of American cities and his unfavorable comparison of Brooklyn to the small town he had left supported the published impressions of Pecorini and emerged as a common theme in the recollections of other repatriates. Salvatore Corvo, who returned to Palermo after four years in Detroit between 1909 and 1913, reported that when he first saw the Michigan city he could not believe that so many people could be in one place.[24] "It was never like that in Corleone," Corvo marveled.[25] He maintained that he had adapted quickly to his new life in the big city, that he found everything in America "*molto bello*" and that he would have gone back to Detroit after World War I if his passport had been renewed. When asked why he returned to Sicily if he liked Michigan so much, he replied, "Oh there was a girl here who kept writing me so I came back to see her. But once I saw her I decided that I didn't want to marry her so the trip was all for nothing."[26]

When Corvo was requested to list what had impressed him most about Detroit as a young man in his teens, he replied that he had noticed that everybody had a plan for his life. "Most of the

---

[23] *Ibid.*
[24] Salvatore Corvo [pseud.] to author, June 17, 1971.
[25] *Ibid.*
[26] *Ibid.*

young men I met in Detroit," he said, "had thought about what they wanted to do, what kind of jobs they meant to get and how they wanted to live. They expected it all to come true, too. I, myself, had never even thought about such long-range things."[27]

Both Antonio Colella and Salvatore Corvo had lived in the United States for only a few years in their youth, and neither man illustrated the divided loyalty that Conte and Carito had noted. Corvo expressed pride in having seen America, but he spoke of himself as a Sicilian with no ties to the second country.

In Bagnoli del Trigno, a small town southeast of Rome, the divided loyalties emerged readily, especially in interviews with recently returned repatriates who had spent many years in the United States. Roberto Foglia, the owner of a coffee shop, related the story of his life spent between two countries. He had made one trip to America and returned to Bagnoli del Trigno before 1914.[28] After the end of the war he left his wife and baby daughter to go to West Virginia where he remained for eight years. In 1929 he returned to Italy after he had lost his total savings of $4,200 in a bank that had failed. "That was a lot of money then," he noted, "more like ten or 15 thousand dollars today."[29]

Foglia returned to Bagnoli del Trigno bitter over the bank failure that had cost him his carefully saved fortune, but he was surprised to find himself dissatisfied with life in the small town. After a year he set out once again for the United States, and for the next 38 years he continued this back and forth migration between the two countries. For three, five or seven years he worked in the United States and saved his dollars. Then he returned to his *paese* for two or three years to see his family, relax and realize how much he missed his other country. In 1968 he retired to Bagnoli del Trigno.

"It's difficult to come back," Foglia said. "You miss the conveniences. All the friends I once had here [in Bagnoli del Trigno] are dead or they have emigrated. Nobody is here to discuss with me the things I have seen and want to talk about. I have had many experiences that I cannot share with them. But I finally decided that my daughter and two granddaughters, the only family I have, are here and I want to spend the last days of my life with them."[30]

---

[27] *Ibid.*
[28] Roberto Foglia [pseud.] to author, July 23, 1971.
[29] *Ibid.*
[30] *Ibid.*

In addition to his divided loyalties, Foglia illustrated what emerged as the common pattern of motivation among repatriates. He had gone to the United States for economic reasons, and he had returned because of family ties. His townsmen reported that Foglia constantly made references to his life in America and spoke English in Bagnoli del Trigno whenever he had the opportunity.

Three of Foglia's *paesani* had also lived in America before 1914, and two of them had settled in the same West Virginia town to which Foglia had gone. In a typical arrangement common to all small towns with large emigration to the western hemisphere, Bagnoli del Trigno had its twin city in America, the place where its early emigrants generally headed at least on their first trip abroad. Those who had already found jobs and housing were expected to help the newly arrived. Most of the emigrants from Bagnoli del Trigno, even those who eventually settled in other parts of America, had gone first to Fairmont, West Virginia, to work in the glass factories.

Riccardo DiGiacomo, a retired iron worker, reported that he left Bagnoli del Trigno the first time in 1909 when he was 15 years old.[31] He stayed in Fairmont only two years on that trip and could remember no specific reason for going back to Italy except to see his family. After visiting with them for a year, DiGiacomo returned to the United States and continued to live in one country and then the other for the next 50 years. Retired in the little town where he was born, he pointed proudly to the two houses he had bought with money earned in America.

Giuseppe Moscarolo, a much older resident of the same town, reported that he had sailed to New York in 1907 when he was 27.[32] He returned to Italy two years later to buy a house and find a wife. After three other work periods in Fairmont, West Virginia, Moscarolo settled in Bagnoli del Trigno in 1924 because his passport was not renewed during the Italian government's curb on emigration.

When asked what effect those years in the United States had had on him and how they had changed his life, Moscarolo tapped the wall of the house behind him. "America bought this house," he

---

[31] Riccardo DiGiacomo [pseud.] to author, July 23, 1971.
[32] Giuseppe Moscarolo [pseud.] to author, July 23, 1971.

said, "something that I never could have owned if I had remained here."[33]

Requested to describe the chief contrasts he had found between his two countries, Moscarolo replied, "The main difference was bread. There was always bread in America."[34]

Moscarolo's elder townsman, Eugenio Buzasi, reported that he had gone to New York only once in 1906 when he was 33 years old.[35] He was summoned back to Bagnoli del Trigno in 1912 in order to divide an estate and never returned to America, one of the few interviewed who made only one trip. During the seven years he spent in New York Buzasi performed all kinds of jobs including work in the sewers for 13 months. He recalled that whatever kind of labor he performed, he earned $1.50 a day, the exact amount mentioned by all the returnees in discussing their pre-1914 experiences in the United States. By watching his expenditures carefully, Buzasi reported, he managed to save 40 or 50 cents a day.

"It was not the America of today," the 98-year-old Buzasi concluded. "We helped to civilize her. But America gave us a lot too."[36] He motioned to the houses of the towns. "America bought most of these houses, and the people who now talk badly about America ought to remember what she did for us."[37]

The experiences related by the repatriates to Bagnoli del Trigno did not differ from those of persons living in other small towns in southern Italy. Divided loyalties, gratitude, pride and a sense of having made a necessary sacrifice emerged in interviews in Mola di Bari and in Molfetta.

Mola di Bari, located on the Adriatic coast eight miles south of the larger city from which it takes its name, formed a club of returned *Americani*. Signs in English and Italian, flags of both countries and photographs of leading figures on both continents indicate members' divided patriotism. Most men in the club in 1971 had traveled to the United States for the first time after World War I and had worked until they became eligible for retirement benefits. Then they had come back to collect in the town they had known only in their youth.

---

[33] *Ibid.*
[34] *Ibid.*
[35] Eugenio Buzasi [pseud.] to author, July 23, 1971.
[36] *Ibid.*
[37] *Ibid.*

The founder of the club, Rinaldo Molina, recalled that he saw New York for the first time in 1907 when he was 17 years old.[38] His brother, who had already settled in America, had called him to come and help earn money for the family back in Mola di Bari. He and his brother, he remembered, went to Seattle, Washington, where he worked as a section boss on the railroad. By cooking for himself and living with other Italian workers, Molina saved one-third of the $1.50 that he earned each day. He pointed out that his savings resulted from great sacrifice unlike "the young men who emigrate today and find a job immediately and a house ready for them."[39] He sent money home at the end of each month in a postal money order.

In 1914 when Molina returned to Italy he missed most the conveniences of Seattle, especially running water in the house. "Having running water out of a faucet changes so much the way you live," he noted. "Certainly a man who lives with plenty of water can be cleaner and more comfortable than one who has to go down to the town fountain for a bucket of water when he needs it. Even now [1971] houses with running water in Mola di Bari don't get water except for two or three hours each day."[40]

After serving in World War I Molina chose to return to the United States where he resumed the job that he had held before leaving. For the next 30 years he lived in America and dreamed of returning to Italy.

Molina reflected on the changes in his life as a result of his stay in the United States: "America changed my life only economically and anyone who is looking for great political or social or religious conversions in those of us who came back will not find them. We went to America to make money and that objective kept us outside politics, religion and the family life of most Americans. We simply were not interested in any of that and since we were not interested, America could not change us."[41]

Pasquale Cecere, another repatriate to Mola di Bari, reported that he made the first of many trips to the United States in 1912.[42] He returned two years later because of the war. Cecere seemed to

---

[38] Rinaldo Molina [pseud.] to author, July 24, 1971.
[39] *Ibid.*
[40] *Ibid.*
[41] *Ibid.*
[42] Pasquale Cecere [pseud.] to author, July 24, 1971.

consider America not an unusual place for a southern Italian to work. He implied that the effect on him had been slight, almost as a man from the suburbs might explain that his job in a downtown office had not affected significantly his view of life. His answers echoed those of most other repatriates both in the words he used and in his surprise at being asked.

Referring to this reason for going abroad as obvious, Cecere said, "There were no jobs here."

And implying that his return to Mola di Bari was just as easily explained, he added, "But my family stayed here."[43]

Molfetta, located about 40 miles north of Mola di Bari, formed its own *Retired USA* club with 34 members who had all lived in the United States and repatriated to Italy. The president of the group, Aldo Branchi, insisted that his long residence in America had caused him to drink only whisky, a habit which amazed his friends and relatives who had never been to the United States.[44] Like the majority of the club's members, he first went to America after World War I and worked long enough to be eligible for retirement benefits which he then elected to receive in Italy. He collected both social security and a pension from his iron worker's job in Hoboken, New Jersey. "Almost all of us who went to the United States from Molfetta settled in Hoboken," he pointed out.[45]

Branchi was enthusiastic about the superiority of the American political system, because he explained, "In the United States there are two parties so that only one is in power at one time. If you don't like what it is doing you vote the other party in. Here in Italy nobody can understand who is in and who is out. There in America everybody participates."[46]

In summarizing the effect his American residence had on him, Branchi compared his life with that of his brother who had never left Molfetta. "I have progressed," Branchi said. "I have lived well. I have been able to send my children to good schools so that today they hold positions of respect. My brother cannot say this."[47]

Roberto Albanese, an earlier Molfetta emigrant to the United States, recalled that his brother had invited him to Hoboken in

---

[43] *Ibid.*
[44] Aldo Branchi [pseud.] to author, July 29, 1971.
[45] *Ibid.*
[46] *Ibid.*
[47] *Ibid.*

1907 when he was 18.[48] His first stay in America lasted three years and during that time he attended school for two months, one of the very few to report any formal education in the United States. He said that he had learned a little English but that he could neither read nor write the language. Albanese returned to Italy because his family was there even though he concluded: "Life in America was very superior. There was always work in America."[49]

Of all the returnees interviewed only Albanese admitted experiencing any prejudice in the United States because of his nationality. He said that he felt the Germans dealt less well with him than they should have. All his countrymen reported that their treatment had been as good as that given any other group of workers.

Albanese was also the only person interviewed who reported observing any irregularities in American political activities. Except Albanese, each man interviewed insisted vehemently that he had observed no buying of votes or other illegal campaign activities. Albanese recalled that once when he went to vote he found that somebody had already signed for him and had cast his ballot. Although he reported the incident to several authorities he never learned what had happened. His conclusion was that there was some corruption in American politics "just like everywhere else."[50]

Antonio Motto, an emigrant from Molfetta in 1905 who returned the first time three years later, concluded that the most important differences for him between the two countries were the school system and the "way people treated each other."[51]

"Here in Italy," Motto said, "if I go into an office or a shop, it's *Dottore* here or *Commendatore* there. In America everybody is Mister."[52]

Motto admitted that he had never attended an American school, but he said that he had insisted that his children attend university in the United States "where they had more chance."[53]

The repatriates whose experiences were available illustrated a set of common experiences and impressions which, although stated

---

[48] Roberto Albanese [pseud.] to author, July 29, 1971.
[49] *Ibid.*
[50] *Ibid.*
[51] Antonio Motto [pseud.] to author, July 29, 1971.
[52] *Ibid.*
[53] *Ibid.*

in another vocabulary, did not differ significantly from that presented in the published accounts of the more educated immigrants and professional observers. Without exception the repatriates listed economic reasons for going to the United States and emotional attachments drawing them back to Italy. They praised the industrial system which furnished work paying as much as ten times what they had formerly earned in their home country, but they criticized the chaos and confusion of the cities in which the jobs were located. Few of the men expressed any belief that life in North America had made them more active politically, although they praised the wider participation in elections which they observed. Several of the returnees spoke enthusiastically of the educational system in the United States, but very few had enrolled for classes. Each one maintained, with one exception, that he suffered no discrimination because of his nationality, eating habits or frugal living arrangements. Each one sought to emphasize that later immigrants to the United States had had an easier time than he had experienced. All of them boasted of having been a part of America's development. Whether they stayed two years or 40, they admitted they were proud they had gone.

The repatriates all spoke of their own personal benefits from working in America, and no one referred to the effect of the remittances or the reemigration on Italy. The men related the amounts they had earned and what they had been able to buy. They boasted of their proficiency in English and the effect of their stories on their *paesani*. No one spoke of his migration and return as the result of anyone's planning except his own, and no one seemed to regret his decision to seek what appeared to him a suitable and profitable arrangement in which he left his family in Italy and went to work in America.

5

Conclusions

THE RETURN to Italy between 1900 and 1914 of some 1.5 million men after temporary residence in the United States brought potentially important consequences for the persons involved, for their compatriots who never had made the journey and for the country they reentered. If, as several advocates of the term have insisted, an American character or spirit exists, then exposure to it possibly affected Europeans living there. Henry Bamford Parkes, the distinguished British-born historian and an ardent supporter of the view that the United States developed in a particular way because of the people who settled it and the resources of its land, wrote:

> [I believe] that American civilization has certain unique features that differentiate it from that of any European country. The culture of the United States has been the product of two main factors: of the impulses and aspirations that caused men and women to leave their European homes and cross the Atlantic; and of the influences of the American natural environment.[1]

Parkes enumerated some of what he considered to be particularly evident American values: an emphasis on developing an agrarian democracy in which all men could own their own land, a stress on individual worth and on the importance of individual freedom, a dislike of authoritarianism, a belief in the supremacy of will, and others.[2]

The evidence examined above does not lead to the conclusion that Italian repatriates perceived any great changes in themselves as a result of residence in the United States between 1900 and 1914. The Italian Council on Emigration pointed to slight changes in the *Americani:* hygiene levels rose, some crime rates decreased and political awareness increased. The one big change for Italy, however, was economic. Temporary residence in the United States did not cause significant political, social, religious or psychological transformations. It provided, however, a solution for economic problems which the emigrants and their country faced.

After 1900 unemployment, underemployment, strikes and other labor disruptions left an army of Italian males searching for jobs or better paying work. According to Epicarmo Corbino, author of a multi-volume economic history of Italy, nearly one-third of

---

[1] Henry Bamford Parkes, *The American Experience* (New York, 1947), x.
[2] *Ibid., passim.*

Italian males above nine years of age worked by the day in the fields in 1901.[3] "This meant," Corbino wrote, "that two million laborers had occasional work and the average pay of this group did not leave any margin to meet the rapidly rising prices of the absolute necessities."[4] He concluded that his government's unwillingness to look for solutions within the country caused mounting dissatisfaction. This resulted in a series of labor stoppages and strikes which recurred with increasing severity after the turn of the century.[5] Between 1901 and 1914 Italy experienced, according to Corbino, 2,957 strikes involving nearly 1.5 million workers.[6] In one year only of that period, 1901, the country was beset by 1,402 strikes and lost 2,146,000 work days.[7] Table XXVII shows that the entire peninsula suffered from labor difficulties.

TABLE XXVII

SHARE OF TOTAL STRIKES AND PARTICIPANTS
IN VARIOUS REGIONS OF ITALY,
1901-1914

Region	Percentage of Strikes	Percentage of Strikers
Emilia	23.2	35.7
Piedmont	17.3	11.5
Lombardy	32.2	15.4
Veneto	10.1	6.5
Apulia	6.0	18.3
Other Areas	11.2	12.6

Epicarmo Corbino, *Annali dell'Economia Italiana* (5 vols., Città di Castello, 1938), V, 456.

Temporary emigration to the western hemisphere removed from the scene hundreds of thousands of laborers each year and took them to jobs paying as much as ten times what they had earned in Italy. Most of them emigrated as single individuals, and the savings they carefully accumulated to send back each month to

---

[3] Epicarmo Corbino, *Annali dell'Economia Italiana* (5 vols., Città di Castello, 1938), IV, 67.

[4] *Ibid.*, 68.

[5] *Ibid.*

[6] *Ibid.*, 462.

[7] *Ibid.*

their families and creditors had important consequences both for the recipients and for Italy.

Constantino Ianni, Brazilian-born son of Italian emigrants, claimed that the Italian government's prohibition of subsidized emigration to Brazil after 1902 resulted primarily from economic considerations rather than from an interest in the welfare of migrating workers.[8] Those who had chosen to go to Brazil typically had taken their families since their contracts with Brazilian companies provided passage for wives and children. Ianni wrote:

> Formally the prohibition [against paid emigration to Brazil] was justified by the worsened conditions of work on the coffee plantations where even the payment of wages was subject to delay. It is, however, a fact that entire families emigrated to Brazil. Therefore small remittances. With the suspension of aided emigration to Brazil, the migratory movement turned toward the United States with the departure of single workers rather than entire families. As a result, the volume of remittances from North America increased considerably.[9]

Ianni did not prove conclusively that the Italian government's motivation for ending aided expatriation to Brazil was economic rather than humanitarian. He showed, however, that remittances from the United States after 1902 increased considerably. This occurred at the same time that large numbers of men began to choose to go to North America instead of Brazil.[10] Others, besides Ianni, had observed a connection between temporary migration and remittances. The Commissariat of Emigration had repeatedly reported in the *Bulletin* that remittances decreased as emigration became more permanent.[11]

Not all the money sent back to Italy went to feed and clothe families left there or to buy land and houses. Bank deposits held in Italy by its citizens residing abroad grew nearly tenfold between 1901 and 1914, indicating that many of the emigrants chose to save their money rather than spend it. Table XXVIII compares the total credit held by Italians resident in another country with that

---

[8] Constantino Ianni, *Il Sangue degli Emigranti* (Milan, 1965), 181.
[9] *Ibid.*
[10] *Ibid.*
[11] Commissariato Generale dell'Emigrazione, *Bollettino dell'Emigrazione,* no. 2 (1902), 30.

possessed by their compatriots at home. Table XXVIII also shows that while deposits held by Italians abroad multiplied nearly ten times, accounts credited to Italians residing in the peninsula grew less than 300 percent.

TABLE XXVIII

LIRE HELD IN ITALIAN BANKS BY ITALIANS RESIDENT IN ITALY AND ABROAD

End of Calendar Year	Held by Residents in Italy	Held by Residents Abroad
1901	684,304,917.11	22,325,025.69
1902	734,258,303.25	35,413,638.00
1903	794,044,176.00	59,954,813.66
1904	873,889,898.25	90,994,792.01
1905	921,904,042.01	127,210,355.98
1906	1,005,568,354.19	184,134,799.77
1907	1,129,383,965.46	264,956,500.79
1908	1,161,183,632.48	320,949,392.84
1909	1,186,758,486.98	369,144,637.47
1910	1,636,156,367.95	107,279,058.19
1911	1,687,415,896.70	153,012,786.22
1912	1,734,113,961.43	183,186,535.92
1913	1,840,219,868.20	219,403,721.51
1914	1,758,032,448.95	215,694,495.73

Commissariato Generale dell'Emigrazione, *Annuario Statistico della Emigrazione, Italiana dal 1876-1925* (Rome, 1926), 1652.

Remittances by temporarily absent workers helped Italy solve the problem of an unfavorable balance of trade during the period 1900 to 1914. During these 15 years Italy's exports never equalled its imports. Corbino estimated that exports from the peninsula amounted to between 62.2 and 84.4 percent of imports in the years 1901 to 1913.[12] The total value of Italy's exports and imports during those years is shown in Table XXIX.

The balance of trade deficit occurred in spite of increased buying of Italian products abroad, stimulated in part by nationals working in other countries. Men living in New York or San Francisco continued to cook and eat much as they had done in their native land. The resulting flow of *pasta*, wine, olive oil and other familiar items sought by the emigrants helped Italy develop its

---

[12] Corbino, *Annali dell' Economia Italiana*, V, 192.

TABLE XXIX

VALUE OF EXPORTS FROM ITALY AND
IMPORTS TO ITALY: 1901-1913°
(IN MILLION OF *LIRE*)

Year	Exports	Imports	Exports as % of Imports
1901	1422	1698	83.6
1902	1469	1768	83.0
1903	1463	1825	80.0
1904	1559	1847	84.4
1905	1666	1996	83.4
1906	1801	2337	76.9
1907	1736	2556	67.9
1908	1672	2698	62.6
1909	1770	2847	62.2
1910	1893	2926	64.9
1911	1982	3019	65.6
1912	2155	3180	67.8
1913	2233	3122	71.5

Based on Epicarmo Corbino, *Annali dell'Economia Italiana* (5 vols., Città di Castello, 1938), V, 192.
°   Excluding precious metals.

markets abroad. Ianni reported that Italian exports to the United States nearly tripled in the first fifteen years of the twentieth century, thus adding support to the saying "Trade follows the emigrant."[13] Ianni also noted that both North and South America increased importations from Italy between 1900 and 1914 in excess of those reported to other parts of Europe. While exports to Brazil and Argentina nearly quadrupled and those to the United States almost tripled, European countries increased their purchases from Italy by 150 percent.[14] Ianni wrote:

As can be seen, the index of the increase of exports to the principal countries of destination for Italian emigrants in the period 1901 to 1913 is considerably superior to that of the total exports to Europe . . . . The problem is not diverse [in 1965].[15]

---

[13] Ianni, *Il Sangue degli Emigranti*, 249.
[14] *Ibid.*, 248.
[15] *Ibid.*

Nationals working outside their country who funneled their savings back to their families and bank accounts not only helped Italy meet its balance of trade difficulties and increase its foreign markets but also contributed to the growth of Italian shipping. Emilio Bettini, the Italian economist and writer, concluded in his study of shipping companies that emigrants played a significant part in that development:

> The transoceanic migration of Italians constitutes, therefore, one of the principal causes of the existence of our large passenger transportation companies such as the Italian line and the Lloyd Triestino with ships among the biggest and most modern in the world.[16]

Bettini noted that Italian emigrants traveling back and forth across the Atlantic benefited not only their own country's shipping lines but also those of France, Germany and the United States.[17] He did not argue, however, that the passengers saw ocean transportation as anything other than a service to their ambitions to work in America.

In their writings and interviews the repatriates never referred to their own contributions to the development of their country's shipping industry and its markets abroad or to the solution of Italy's balance of payments deficit and unemployment problems. If they considered their temporary emigration an important component of Italy's answer to multiple problems encountered between 1900 and 1914, these views did not emerge from their writings and recollections. The returnees appeared oblivious to the various groups who gained from the sacrifices the emigrants made when they left their families in Italy and sought work in North America.

The Italian government, on the other hand, had a well-developed idea of the importance of its temporary emigrants. It attempted to increase periodic migration by publicizing its approval of repatriation, by easing requirements for resumption of Italian citizenship, by subsidizing organizations which fostered ties between emigrants and their home country and by providing discounts on parts of the return trip.

---

[16] Emilio Bettini, "Alcuni Aspetti Economici dell'Emigrazione Italiana," *Homo Faber*, VII (August 1956), 3558.
[17] *Ibid.*

The returnees recounted their adventures in the United States with pride and some amusement at the confusion they experienced adapting to a new country. Some men spoke of civilizing the United States and of helping it reach present strength, but each worker emphasized America's contribution to his own economic well-being and to the property he had accumulated.

The residents of small Italian towns who welcomed back workers from the United States may have observed slight differences in the repatriates' manner of dressing, amount of gold dental work or vocabulary, leading them to call the returnees *Americani*. The only important change for the men coming back was in their bank accounts. For their co-workers, neighbors and elected officials the repatriates may have been temporary Americans but in their own opinions they remained Italians.

6

Bibliography

GOVERNMENT DOCUMENTS: ITALY AND THE UNITED STATES

Beneduce, Alberto, "Saggio di Statistica dei Rimpatriati dalle Americhe," in Commissariato Generale dell'Emigrazione, *Bollettino dell'Emigrazione*, no. 11 (1911), 1-103.

Commissariato Generale dell'Emigrazione. *Annuario Statistico dell'Emigrazione Italiana* (Rome, 1926).

Commissariato Generale dell'Emigrazione. *Bollettino dell'Emigrazione* (Rome, 1902 to 1915).

Commissariato Generale dell'Emigrazione. *L'Emigrazione Italiana* (Rome, 1925).

Correnti, Cesare. *Annuario Statistico Italiano, 1854-58* (Turin, 1858).

Direzione Generale della Statistica. *Statistica della Emigrazione Italiana* (Rome, 1896/97 to 1913/14).

Istituto Centrale di Statistica. *Sommario di Statistiche Storiche Italiane: 1861-1955* (Rome, 1958).

U.S. Bureau of the Census. *Statistical Abstract of the Fourteenth Census of the United States, 1920* (Washington, 1923).

U.S. Bureau of the Census. *Statistical History of the United States from Colonial Times to the Present* (Washington, 1966).

U.S. Bureau of the Census. *Thirteenth Census of the United States Taken in the Year 1910: Abstract of the Census* (Washington, 1913).

U.S. Commissioner General of Immigration. *Annual Report* (Washington, 1891/2 to 1913/14).

U.S. Immigration Commission, 1907-1910. *Reports of the Immigration Commission* (41 vols., Washington, 1911).

U.S. Industrial Commission. *The Commission's Reports* (15 vols., Washington, 1901).

MEMOIRS, DIARIES AND LETTERS

Bagot, Richard. *My Italian Year* (London, 1911).

Barbera, Piero. *Editori e Autori: Studi e Passatempi di un Libraio* (Florence, 1904).

Carito, Diomede. *Nella Terra di Washington: Le Mie Visioni della Psiche Nord Americana* (Naples, 1912).

Ciarlantini, Franco. *Al Paese delle Stelle* (Milan, 1931).

Conte, Gaetano. *Dieci Anni in America* (Milan, 1903).

Corsi, Edward. *In the Shadow of Liberty* (New York, 1935).

Ferreri, Gherardo. *Gli Italiani in America* (Rome, 1907).

Hooton, Charles. *St. Louis' Isle* (London, 1847).

Panunzio, Constantine. *The Soul of the Immigrant* (New York, 1921).

Rossi, Louis. *Six Ans en Amerique* (Paris, 1863).

OTHER UNPUBLISHED WORKS

Bjork, Robert. "The Italian Immigration into France: 1870-1954" (Unpublished Ph.D. Dissertation, Syracuse University, 1955).

Carter, John Booth. "American Reactions to Italian Fascism, 1913-1933" (Unpublished Ph.D. Dissertation, Columbia University, 1953).

Cerase, Francesco. "From Italy to the United States and Back" (Unpublished Ph.D. Dissertation, Columbia University, 1971).

Dijour, Ilja. "Seminar on the Integration of Immigrants" (Unpublished Report of the American Immigration and Citizenship Conference, New York, 1960).

Fenton, Edwin. "Immigrants and Unions: A Case Study of Italians and American Labor, 1870-1920" (Unpublished Ph.D. Dissertation, Harvard, 1957).

Iorizzo, L. J. "Italian Immigration and the Impact of the Padrone System" (Unpublished Ph.D. Dissertation, Syracuse University, 1966).

Knuth, Helen Elizabeth. "The Climax of American Anglo-Saxonism, 1898-1905" (Unpublished Ph.D. Dissertation, Northwestern, 1958).

Kolm, R. "The Change of Cultural Identity: An Analysis of Factors Conditioning the Cultural Integration of Immigrants" (Unpublished Ph.D. Dissertation, Wayne State, 1966).

Krueger, Nancy Moore. "Assimilation and Adjustment of Postwar Immigrants in Franklin County, Ohio" (Unpublished Ph.D. Dissertation, Ohio State, 1955).

Matthews, M. F. "The Role of the Public School in the Assimilation of the Italian Immigrant Child in New York City, 1900-1914" (Unpublished Ph.D. Dissertation, Fordham, 1966).

Nelli, H.S. "The Role of the 'Colonial' Press in the Italian-American Community of Chicago, 1866-1921" (Unpublished Ph.D. Dissertation, University of Chicago, 1966).

Parenti, Michael J. "Ethnic and Political Attitudes: A Depth Study of Italian-Americans" (Unpublished Ph.D. Dissertation, Yale, 1962).

Schrier, Arnold. "Ireland and the American Emigration: 1850-1900" (Unpublished Ph.D. Dissertation, Northwestern, 1956).

Valletta, C. L. "A Study of Americanization in Carnetta: Italian-American Identity Through Three Generations" (Unpublished Ph.D. Dissertation, University of Pennsylvania, 1968).

Winsey, V.R. "A Study of the Effect of Transplantation upon the Attitudes Toward the United States of Southern Italians in New York City as Revealed by Survivors of the Mass Migration, 1887-1915" (Unpublished Ph. D. Dissertation, New York University, 1966).

INTERVIEWS

Albanese, Roberto [pseud.]. Molfetta, Italy. July 29, 1971.
Albano, Cristoforo [pseud.]. Enna, Italy. June 24, 1971.
Bacchi, Giovanni [pseud.]. Mola, Italy. July 24, 1971.
Branchi, Aldo [pseud.]. Molfetta, Italy. July 29, 1971.
Buzasi, Eugenio [pseud.]. Bagnoli del Trigno, Italy. July 23, 1971.
Cecere, Pasquale [pseud.]. Mola di Bari, Italy. July 24, 1971.
Ciavarello, Gino. Palermo, Italy. June 15, 1971.
Colella, Gaetano [pseud.]. Agrigento, Italy. June 23, 1971.
Corvo, Salvatore [pseud.]. Palermo, Italy. June 17, 1971.
Di Giacomo, Riccardo [pseud.]. Bagnoli del Trigno, Italy. July 23, 1971.
Donato, Franco [pseud.]. Siracusa, Italy. June 26, 1971.
Foglia, Roberto [pseud.]. Bagnoli del Trigno, Italy. July 23, 1971.
Gentile, Antonio [pseud.]. Mola di Bari, Italy. July 24, 1971.
Grano, Vincenzo [pseud.]. Molfetta, Italy. July 29, 1971.
Librizzi, Antonio [pseud.]. Agrigento, Italy. June 23, 1971.
Macarocci, Anna. Rome, Italy. July 6, 1971.

Manzin, Vittorio. Venice, Italy. July 11, 1971.
Milanulli, Nunzio [pseud.]. Mola di Bari, Italy. July 24, 1971.
Molina, Rinaldo [pseud.]. Mola di Bari, Italy. July 24, 1971.
Moscarolo, Giuseppe [pseud.]. Bagnoli del Trigno, Italy. July 23, 1971.
Motto, Antonio [pseud.]. Molfetta, Italy. July 29, 1971.
Petrucci, Ettore. Rome, Italy. July 5, 1971.
Pinto, Vincenzo [pseud.]. Erice, Italy. June 21, 1971.
Randazzo, Franco [pseud.]. Palermo, Italy. June 17, 1971.
Rossi, Domenico. Rome, Italy. June 1, 1971.
Tito, Giuseppe. Bari, Italy. May 7, 1971.
Villani, Giovanni [pseud.]. Molfetta, Italy. July 29, 1971.
Viso, Teodorico [pseud.]. Mola di Bari, Italy. July 24, 1971.
Zucco, Giuseppe [pseud.]. Erice, Italy. June 21, 1971.

SECONDARY WORKS

Baden, Anne L. *Immigration in the United States* (Washington, 1943).
Bongiorno, Arrigo and Barbina, Aldo. *Il Pane degli Altri* (Milan, 1971).
Borrie, W. D. *The Cultural Integration of Immigrants* (Paris, 1959).
Branchi, Eugenio Camillo. *Il Primato degli Italiani nella Storia e nella Civiltà Americana* (Bologna, 1925).
Brown, Lawrence Guy. *Immigration: Cultural Conflicts and Social Adjustments* (New York, 1933).
Cabrini, Angiolo. *Il Maestro degli Emigranti* (Imola, 1912).
Carpenter, Niles. *Immigrants and Their Children, 1920* (Washington, 1927).
Carpi, Leone. *Delle Colonie e dell'Emigrazione d'Italiani all'Estero* (4 vols., Milan, 1874).
Carpi, Leone. *Dell'Emigrazione Italiana all'Estero* (Florence, 1871).
Carr, John Foster. *Guida degli Stati Uniti* (Garden City, 1910).
Carr, John Foster. *The Italian Immigrant Looks at the Future* (New York, 1918).
Cerase, Francesco. *L'Emigrazione di Ritorno* (Rome, 1971).
Child, Irwin. *Italian or American: The Second Generation Conflict* (New Haven, 1943).
Commager, Henry Steele, ed. *Immigration and American History* (Minneapolis, 1961).
Commons, John. *Races and Immigrants in America* (New York, 1907).
Corbino, Epicarmo. *Annali dell' Economia Italiana* (5 vols., Citta di Castello, 1938).
Davie, Maurice R. *World Immigration* (New York, 1936).
Davis, Philip, ed. *Immigration and Americanization* (New York, 1920).
Dickinson, Robert. *The Population Problem of Southern Italy* (Syracuse, 1955).
Duval, Jules. *Histoire de l'Emigration Europeene, Asiatique et Africaine au XIXe Siècle* (Paris, 1862).
Eisenstadt, S. N. *The Absorption of Immigrants* (Glencoe, 1955).
Eisenstadt, S. N. *From Generation to Generation* (Glencoe, 1956).
Ernst, Robert. *Immigrant Life in New York City: 1825-1863* (New York, 1949).
Facenna, D. Filippo. *Per i Nostri Emigranti al di là dell' Oceano* (Tivoli, 1914).
Ferber, Nat J. *A New American* (New York, 1938).
Florenzano, Giovanni. *Della Emigrazione Italiana in America* (Naples, 1874).
Foerster, Robert F. *The Italian Emigration of Our Times* (Cambridge, 1919).
Franzoni, Ausonia. *Gli Italiani d'America e la Cittadinanza* (Rome, 1923).

Garlick, Richard C. et al. Italy and the Italians in Washington's Time (New York, 1933).

Gerson, Louis L. The Hyphenates in Recent American Politics and Diplomacy (Lawrence, 1964).

Glazer, Nathan and Moynihan, Daniel Patrick. Beyond the Melting Pot (Cambridge, 1963).

Goggio, Emilio. Italians in American History (New York, 1930).

Gordon, Milton M. Assimilation in American Life (New York, 1964).

Grebler, Leo. Housing Market Behavior in a Declining Area (New York, 1952).

Handlin, Oscar. Immigration as a Factor in American History (Englewood Cliffs, 1959).

Handlin, Oscar. The Uprooted (New York, 1951).

Handlin, Oscar. "The Immigrant and American Politics," in David F. Bowers, ed., Foreign Influences in American Life (Princeton, 1944), 117-30.

Higham, John. Strangers in the Land (New Brunswick, 1955).

Hutchinson, Edward P. Immigrants and their Children: 1850-1950 (New York, 1956).

Ianni, Constantino. Il Sangue degli Emigranti (Milan, 1965).

Iorizzo, Luciano J. and Mondello, Salvatore. The Italian-Americans (New York, 1971).

Jerome, Harry. Migration and Business Cycles (New York, 1926).

Jones, Maldwyn Allen. American Immigration (Chicago, 1960).

Kuznets, Simon and Rubin, Ernest. Immigration and the Foreign Born (New York, 1954).

Livi Bacci, Massimo. L'Immigrazione e l'Assimilazione degli Italiani negli Stati Uniti—Seconde le Statistiche Demografiche Americane (Milan, 1961).

Lopreato, Joseph. Italian Americans (New York, 1970).

Lopreato, Joseph. Peasants No More (San Francisco, 1967).

Lord, Eliot, ed. The Italian in America (New York, 1905).

Luebke, Frederick C. Immigrants and Politics: The Germans in Nebraska, 1880-1900 (Lincoln, 1969).

McDonagh, Edward C. and Richards, Eugene. Ethnic Relations in the United States (New York, 1953).

Mangano, Antonio. Sons of Italy: A Social and Religious Study of Italians in America (New York, 1917).

Mangione, Jerre. Mount Allegro (Boston, 1942).

Mariano, John Horace. Second Generation Italians in New York City (Boston, 1921).

Musmanno, Michael A. The Story of Italians in America (New York, 1965).

Nelli, Humbert S. Italians in Chicago, 1880-1930 (New York, 1970).

Palma di Castiglione, G. L'Immigrazione Italiana negli Stati Uniti dell'America del Nord dal 1820 al 30 Giugno, 1910 (Rome, 1913).

Park, Robert E. An Outline of the Principles of Sociology (New York, 1939).

Park, Robert E. and Miller, Herbert A. Old World Traits Transplanted (New York, 1921).

Parkes, Henry Bamford. The American Experience (New York, 1947).

Pecorini, Alberto. Gli Americani nella Vita Moderna (Milan, 1909).

Peel, Roy. The Political Clubs of New York (New York, 1935).

Pisani, Lawrence F. The Italian in America (New York, 1957).

Pola, Antonia. Who Can Buy the Stars? (New York, 1957).

Preziosi, Giovanni. Gli Italiani negli Stati Uniti del Nord (Milan, 1909).

Radin, Paul. The Italians of San Francisco (San Francisco, 1935).

Rolle, Andrew F. *The Immigrant Upraised* (Norman, 1968).

Rose, Philip M. *The Italians in America* (New York, 1922).

Roselli, Bruno. *Our Italian Immigrants: Their Racial Backgrounds* (New York, 1927).

Rossi, Luigi. *Relazione sui Servizi dell' Emigrazione per l'Anno, 1909-1910* (Rome, 1910).

Ruggiero, Amerigo. *Italiani in America* (Milan, 1937).

Russo, Giovanni. *Emigrazione dell' Europa e Immigrazione in America e in Australasia* (Rome, 1907).

Saloutos, Theodore. *They Remember America* (Berkeley, 1956).

Santini, Florio. *Italiani nel Mondo* (Massarosa, 1969).

Sartorio, Henry Charles. *Social and Religious Life of Italians in America* (Boston, 1918).

Schiavo, Giovanni. *Four Centuries of Italian-American History* (New York, 1952).

Schiavo, Giovanni. *The Italians in America before the Civil War* (New York, 1934).

Schiavo, Giovanni. *The Italians in Chicago* (Chicago, 1928).

Schiavo, Giovanni. *The Italians in Missouri* (New York, 1929).

Shepperson, Wilbur S. *Emigration and Disenchantment* (Norman, 1965).

Shuval, Judith T. *Immigrants on the Threshold* (New York, 1963).

Smith, William Carlson. *Americans in the Making: The Natural History of the Assimilation of Immigrants* (New York, 1939).

Solomon, Barbara M. *Ancestors and Immigrants* (Boston, 1956).

Stella, Antonio. *Some Aspects of Italian Immigration to the United States* (New York, 1924).

Taeuber, Conrad and Taeuber, Irene. *The Changing Population of the United States* (New York, 1958).

Taft, Donald and Robbins, Richard. *International Migrations* (New York, 1955).

Thompson, W.S. and Whelpton, P.K. *Population Trends in the United States* (New York, 1933).

Ticchioni, Emanuele. *L'Alfabeto dell' Emigrante Transoceanico* (Tivoli, 1914).

Tomasi, Silvano, ed. *The Italian Experience in the United States* (Staten Island, 1970).

Torrielli, Andrew J. *Italian Opinion on America as Revealed by Italian Travelers, 1850-1900* (Cambridge, 1941).

Tyler, Poyntz, ed. *Immigration and the United States* (New York, 1956).

Vagts, Alfred. Deutsch-Amerikanische Rückwanderung: *Probleme, Phänomene, Statistik, Politik, Soziologie, Biographie* (Heidelberg, 1960).

Villari, Luigi. *Gli Stati Uniti d'America e l'Emigrazione Italiana* (Milan, 1912).

Wakefield, Dan. *Island in the City* (Boston, 1959).

Warner, Lloyd and Srole, Leo. *The Social Systems of American Ethnic Groups* (New Haven, 1945).

Whyte, William F. *Street Corner Society: The Social Structure of an Italian Slum* (Chicago, 1943).

Wilder, Thornton. *The Cabala* (New York, 1926).

Willcox, Walter F. *International Migrations* (2 vols., New York, 1929-1931).

Williams, Phyllis H. *South Italian Folkways in Europe and America* (New Haven, 1938).

ARTICLES

Ascoli, Max. "On the Italian-Americans," *Common Ground*, III (Autumn 1942), 45-49.

Bernard, William S. "Integration of Immigrants in the United States," *International Migration Review*, I (Spring 1967), 57-62.

Bettini, Emilio. "Alcuni Aspetti Economici dell'Emigrazione Italiana," *Homo Faber*, VII (August 1956), 3555-560.

Boas, Franz. "The Effects of the American Environment on Immigrants and Their Descendants," *Science*, LXXXIV (1936), 522-25.

Browne, Henry J. "The Italian Problem in the Catholic Church of the United States, 1880-1900," *Historical Records and Studies*, XXXV (1946), 46-75.

Buscemi, Philip A. "The Sicilian Immigrant and His Language Problems," *Sociology and Social Research*, XII (November-December 1927), 137-43.

Campisi, P. J. "Ethnic Family Patterns: The Italian Family in the United States," *American Journal of Sociology*, LIII (May 1948), 443-49.

Carr, John F. "The Coming of the Italian," *Outlook*, LXXXII (February 1906), 419-31.

Carr, John F. "The Italian in the United States," *World's Work*, VIII (October 1904), 5393-5404.

Cerase, Francesco P. "A Study of Italian Migrants Returning from the U.S.A.," *International Migration Review*, I (Summer 1967), 67-74.

Ciampis, Mario de. "Note sul Movimento Socialista tra gli Emigrati Italiani negli Stati Uniti, 1890-1921," *Cronache Meridonali*, VI (April 1959), 255-73.

Cometti, Elizabeth. "Trends in Italian Emigration," *Western Political Quarterly*, XI (December 1958), 820-34.

Cornwell, Elmer E., Jr. "Party Absorption of Ethnic Groups: The Case of Providence, Rhode Island," *Social Forces*, XXXVIII (March 1960), 205-10.

Dickinson, Joan Y. "Aspects of Italian Immigration to Philadelphia," *Pennsylvania Magazine of History and Biography*, XC (October 1966), 445-65.

Duncan, Otis Dudley and Lieberson, Stanley. "Ethnic Segregation and Assimilation," *American Journal of Sociology*, LXIV (January 1959), 364-74.

Feldman, Egal. "Prostitution, the Alien Woman and the Progressive Imagination, 1910-1915," *American Quarterly*, XIX (Summer 1967), 192-206.

Firkins, Ina Ten Eyck. "Italians in the United States," *Bulletin of Bibliography*, VIII (January 1915), 129-33.

Franklin, Lawrence. "The Italian in America: What He Has Been, What He Shall Be," *Catholic World*, LXXI (April 1900), 67-80.

Fuchs, Lawrence. "Minority Groups and Foreign Policy," *Public Opinion Quarterly*, LXXIV (June 1959), 161-75.

Gans, Herbert J. "Some Comments on the History of Italian Migration and on the Nature of Historical Research," *International Migration Review*, I (Summer 1967), 5-9.

Glazer, Nathan. "The Dynamics of Ethnic Identification," *American Sociological Review*, XXIII (1958), 31-40.

Glazer, Nathan. "The Immigrant Groups and American Culture," *Yale Review*, XLVIII (March 1959), 382-97.

Gleason, Philip. "The Melting Pot: Symbol of Fusion or Confusion," *American Quarterly*, XVI (1964), 20-46.

Gordon, Milton M. "Assimilation in America: Theory and Reality," *Daedalus*, XC (Spring 1961), 263-85.

Handlin, Oscar. "Immigrants Who Go Back," Atlantic, CXCVIII (July 1956), 70-74.

Heiss, Jerold. "Factors Related to Immigrant Assimilation: The Early Post-Migration Situation," Human Organization, XXVI (Winter 1967), 265-72.

Heiss, Jerold. "Factors Related to Immigrant Assimilation: Pre-Migration Traits," Social Forces, XLVII (June 1969), 422-28.

Heiss, Jerold. "Residential Segregation and the Assimilation of Italians in an Australian City," International Migration, IV (Spring 1966), 165-71.

Heiss, Jerold. "Sources of Satisfaction and Assimilation Among Italian Immigrants," Human Relations, XIX (May 1966), 165-77.

Higham, John. "Another Look at Nativism," Catholic Historical Review, XLIV (1958), 147-58.

Hutchinson, Edward P. "Notes on Immigration Statistics of the United States," Journal of American Statistical Association, LIII (December 1958), 963-1025.

Levi, Carlo. "Italy's Myth of America," Life, XXIII (July 1947), 84-5.

Lopreato, Joseph. "How Would You Like to be a Peasant?" Human Organization, XXIV (Winter 1965-66), 298-307.

McLaughlin, Allan. "Social and Political Effects of Immigration," Popular Science Monthly, LXVI (January 1905), 243-55.

Mayer, Kurt B. Review of Alfred Vagts, Deutsch-Amerikanische Rückwanderung: Probleme, Phänomene, Statistik, Politik, Soziologie, Biographie in American Sociological Review, XXVI (February 1961), 139-40.

Moss, Leonard. "Ricerche Socio-Culturali di Studiosi Americani," Bollettino delle Ricerche Sociali, I (November 1961), 502-17.

Nahirny, Vladimir and Fishman, Joshua A. "American Immigrant Groups," Sociological Review, XIII (November 1965), 311-26.

Nelli, Humbert S. "Italians in Urban America," International Migration Review, I (Summer 1967), 38-55.

Olin, Spencer C., Jr. "European Immigrant and Oriental Alien," Pacific Historical Review, XXXV (August 1966), 303-15.

Perotti, Antonio. "La Società Italiana di fronte alle Prime Migrazioni di Massa," Studi Emigrazione, V (Spring 1968), 1-196.

Rischin, Moses. "Beyond the Last Divide: Immigration and the Last Frontier," Journal of American History, LV (June 1968), 42-53.

Rolle, Andrew F. "America Through Foreign Eyes," Western Humanities Review, IX (Summer 1955), 261-64.

Rosenthal, Eric. "Acculturation without Assimilation," American Journal of Sociology, LXVI (November 1960), 275-88.

Ross, E.A. "Immigrants in Politics: Political Consequences of Immigration," Century, LXXXVII (January 1914), 392-98.

Sachse, William L. "The Migration of New Englanders to England, 1640-1660," American Historical Review, LIII (January 1948), 251-78.

San Giuliano, Antonio di. "L'Emigrazione Italiana negli Stati Uniti," Nuova Antologia, CXVIII (July-August 1905), 88-104.

Schyler, Eugene. "Italian Immigration in the United States," Political Science Quarterly, IV (September 1889), 480-95.

Smith, Timothy. "New Approaches to the History of Immigration in Twentieth Century America," American Historical Review, LXXI (July 1966), 1265-79.

Spiro, Medford E. "The Acculturation of American Ethnic Groups," American Anthropologist, LVII (December 1955), 1240-52.

Vecoli, R. J. "Contadini in Chicago: A Critique of the Uprooted," *Journal of American History*, LI (December 1964), 404-17.

Willcox, Walter F. "Distribution of Immigrants in the United States," *Quarterly Journal of Economics*, XX (August 1906), 523-46.